D1569688

I Was a Communist for the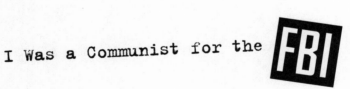

The Pennsylvania State University Press, University Park, Pennsylvania

I Was a Communist for the FBI

The Unhappy Life and Times of Matt Cvetic

Daniel J. Leab

Library of Congress Cataloging-in-Publication Data

Leab, Daniel J.
I was a communist for the F.B.I. : the unhappy life and times of Matt
Cvetic/Daniel J. Leab.
    p.   cm.
Includes bibliographical references and index.
ISBN 0-271-02053-9 (alk. paper)
    1. Cvetic, Matthew, 1909–62. 2. Moles (Spies)–Pennsylvania–Pittsburgh–
Biography. 3. Anti-communist movements–Pennsylvania–Pittsburgh–History–
20th century. 4. Communism–Pennsylvania–Pittsburgh–History–20th century.
5. United States. Federal Bureau of Investigation–Biography. 6. Pittsburgh
(Pa.)–Politics and government–20th century. 7. United States–Politics and
government–1945–1953. 8. Internal security–United States–History–20th
century–Case studies. 9. Anti-communist movements–United States–History–
20th century–Case studies.

F159.P653 C85 2000
974.8'8604'092–dc21
[B]

                                                              00-035660

Copyright © 2000 The Pennsylvania State University
All rights reserved
Printed in the United States of America
Published by The Pennsylvania State University Press,
University Park, PA 16802-1003

It is the policy of The Pennsylvania State University Press to use acid-free paper for
the first printing of all clothbound books. Publications on uncoated stock satisfy the
minimum requirements of American National Standard for Information Sciences–
Permanence of Paper for Printed Library Materials, ANSI Z39.48–1992.

For

Marie-Luise Frings-Wellenreuther

Brave Friend ★ Indomitable Spirit ★ Proud Scholar

She did not "go gentle into that good night."

Contents

Preface

This book has been a long time aborning, almost a decade and a half. University administrative chores, bouts of ill health, and some family problems all have served as temporary roadblocks. The philosopher Pascal once said that "the last thing that we find in making a book is to know what we must put first." I have no such problem. What must be put first is the many who helped to bring this project to fruition.

I owe an enormous debt for their help and advice to the staff at the Carnegie Library in Pittsburgh, the UE/Labor Archives at the University of Pittsburgh, Special Collections at Duquesne University Library, the Catherwood Library at the New York State School of Industrial and Labor Relations (Cornell University), the Firestone Library at Princeton University, the Ziv Papers at the University of Cincinnati, and the Warner Brothers Archive at the University of Southern California.

I am also indebted to the anonymous reviewers at the Federal Bureau of Investigation who were of assistance in making available to me the wide range of Bureau records I obtained under the Freedom of Information Act (FOIA)—at the time I obtained these records the restrictions on release of material were much less than has proved to be the case subsequently, but nonetheless substantial deletions occurred. I requested material on Cvetic from the FBI under the FOIA in July 1988. A first batch of material was released to me in May 1989. Of the 415 pages reviewed by the Bureau, 267 were released, many with substantial deletions. A second batch was released in September 1989, and a third in February 1990: each time there were substantial deletions. Various materials were released over the next two years. Notwithstanding the disappointment occasioned by the deletions I found the FBI reviewers to be helpful, courteous, and concerned. But the guidelines these reviewers were required to follow do vitiate the FOIA. Moreover, and this is an important caveat, 1940/1950 FBI files need to be used with care, given that much of what is available often is hearsay, and also was designed to curry favor with then FBI director J. Edgar Hoover. Despite such caveats, as well as the time-consuming delays encountered in obtaining the FBI material and that found in the files of other government departments I queried, it seems to me that the FOIA remains a very useful tool.

Especially helpful to me in a variety of ways were Terry Belanger (who at a crucial moment made it possible to get access to Pittsburgh newspaper morgues), Lizabeth Gray of *Pittsburgh Post-Gazette* Information Products (who was of great assistance in obtaining the rights to and prints of various illustrations for this book), Monsignor Charles Owen Rice (who despite doubts about the direction of this study facilitated a number of key interviews), David Rosenberg (an invaluable cicerone to the UE archives), Steve Rosswurm (who lent me his FBI files on Harry A. Sherman, Blair Gunther, and other anti-Communist Pittsburghers), Morleen Getz Rouse (who aided my use of the Ziv Papers), Arthur J. Sabin (who shared with me thoughts and material on Cvetic's participation in the decertification of the International Workers Order), Mrs. Harry Alan Sherman (who sent me some material on her late husband's life), and Christine Whittaker (who made available to me BBC shows on the Cold War that allowed me to see Cvetic in action).

In researching this book I contacted many people, a significant number more than once, and probably verged on being a real nuisance. With great generosity and patience, they offered me orientation, insights, and clues—from all of which I much benefited. They did not cavil at my repeated phone calls, letters, faxes, and visits, and accepted my inquiries with goodwill and much forthrightness, even if not always agreeing with what they thought was my point of view. They are named in the chapter notes at the end of the book. And I thank them all, for without their assistance I would not have been able to complete this book.

I am very grateful to those who worked their way through various versions of the manuscript, especially Nick Cull, Tom Doherty, Sidney Fine, John Earl Haynes, and Paul Smith. David Montgomery, who forcefully disagrees with my approach and my conclusions, early on provided guidance and made some very useful comments: I very much regret that he and I have a different take on certain topics covered by this book.

I also much benefited from the comments of the Penn State University readers: one anonymous, and the other, Steve Rosswurm. I am enormously indebted to James Boylan, a good friend, a wise historian, and a marvelous editor, who gave my manuscript a close critical reading and once again saved me from errors of commission and of omission.

The author Erica Jong has correctly stated that "writing is one of the few professions left where you take all responsibility for what you do." And I certainly do—but I would have been seriously remiss in not acknowledging the valued assistance I received from various friends and colleagues.

I also owe a great debt to Seton Hall University, which thanks to a generous sabbatical policy enabled me to spend uninterrupted months researching and writing. A very much different version of some of the material in this book appeared in the *Pennsylvania Magazine of History and Biography,* whose then editor Randall Miller forced me to rethink and to rewrite, with very positive end results. My sincere thanks also go to the Stoessel family (of Pittsburgh) for their assistance over the years. For their intelligent aid at key moments I am indebted to Michelle H. Linver and Steve Karian. Janet Wildman typed up an earlier version of the Cvetic story, and I still appreciate her enjoyment and comments. Over the past decade, Joan-Marie Freitag has done yeoman service in putting onto disk and into type my barely decipherable scrawl; her patience, interest, and good cheer continue to be vital to my efforts, as with the manuscript for this book. Peter Potter of the Penn State University Press showed patience, diligence, and support when it counted—he is an ideal editor.

To all who aided me I give sincere thanks. They have saved me from making blunders of various kinds. For whatever errors of fact or interpretation that may remain, I alone, of course, am responsible.

That I was able to finish the manuscript for this book is due to the ministrations of Drs. Peter Christodolou, O. Wayne Isom, Henry Solomon, and Jeffrey Tyler, as well as the staff and nurses at New Milford Hospital and New York Hospital. I owe a special debt to my friend Justin Ahamad, M.D., but for whom I might be dead.

The Leab children—Abigail, Constance, and Marcus—all put up with inconveniences occasioned by my pursuit of the Cvetic story. They accepted with good grace and fine humor their father's absences and preoccupation. Marcus deserves special mention for exceptional services rendered.

Once upon a time, Van Wyck Brooks (a prescient critic if ever there was one) in a somewhat different context asserted that "no man should ever publish a book until he had first read it to a woman." My wife, Katharine Kyes Leab, has for over three decades listened to what I have written, and saved me from many a folly. Probably by the time this particular manuscript was ready for publication she may have heard it so often as to have memorized it. As always my biggest debt is to her. She is a splendid incisive critic and a good sport (not everyone would have been willing to spend so much time with Matt Cvetic).

Daniel J. Leab
Washington, Connecticut
New York City
January 2000

Introduction

Who is Matt Cvetic? If you've ever heard the phrase "I was a Communist for the FBI," then you have heard of Cvetic, the "I" of the phrase. Because of his impact and notoriety in the early 1950s as a professional anti-Communist, he deserves to be known. Cvetic served as an important governmental resource in diverse deportation and loyalty hearings; he was a key witness in various federal and state attacks on the Communist Party of the United States and some of its "front" organizations; and he testified before a series of federal, state, and extragovernmental local committees.

Today, however, only a few specialized American political and social Cold War histories recognize the man and his impact. As with so many other people who once dominated the newspaper headlines and air waves, Cvetic has receded into what the English novelist L. P. Hartley has called "the foreign country of the past." Cvetic has slipped from the public consciousness and has attracted little scholarly attention. He has received little consideration, for example, in the various histories of Cold War American domestic anti-Communism which appeared during the 1990s and "brought the fight about Communism in America back to life." [1]

As British political scientist K. G. Robertson points out, "The controversy over Communist penetration . . . rages." But Cvetic figures very little in it. Once upon a time, Cvetic was a front-page personage who, justifiably or not, achieved renown and notoriety; he has become almost a nonperson. He should not be forgotten because his story speaks volumes about his era. [2]

Matt Cvetic, at the behest of the FBI, joined a Pittsburgh branch of the CP in 1943. He became one of many such Bureau plants in the Party during the 1940s. Cvetic did manage to become a low-level Party functionary in its western Pennsylvania district. The FBI did find Cvetic to be of some use, and he deserves being dubbed "Pennsylvania's most significant mole." Yet, overall, Cvetic had a limited career both within the Party and in the area's front groups. Ultimately, because of his erratic behavior, the FBI at the beginning of 1950 secretly canned him—a firing that remained unknown for over a generation.[3]

Just why the FBI enlisted Cvetic remains unclear, and the reasons will probably remain lost to history. Certainly nothing in the thirty-plus years of Cvetic's life prior to his recruitment mark him as a man to approach. The product of a typical, somewhat upwardly mobile, lower-middle-class Slavic immigrant family, Cvetic had a limited formal education and a checkered employment record. His marriage and family life left something to be desired, and he had a bit of a drinking problem (which got worse after his service with the FBI).[4] Most of his shortcomings became public knowledge after he surfaced in 1950, as a result of his activities during the first half of the 1950s as a "kept witness"—a term used by journalist Richard Rovere to damn those who made a "business of being witnesses" and thereby "befouling due process." Not always successful efforts to impeach Cvetic's testimony led to numerous attempts to discredit him by exposing his past indiscretions.[5]

The bulk of the kept witnesses proved to be ephemeral heroes, despite their then-lauded stance of combating subversion and the Communist menace. Some did get greater exposure than Cvetic, but he did well. Cvetic was the subject of a multipart series in a popular national magazine (a three-part version of his House Un-American Activities Committee [HUAC] testimony "as told to Pete Martin" appeared in the *Saturday Evening Post*). The series verged on fiction in some segments as the articles explained what "posing as a Communist for the FBI" entailed for Cvetic. He also benefited from the national exposure the *Post* articles occasioned, especially from the sale of the screen rights. Warner Brothers, an important Hollywood studio, brought the Cvetic story to the screen as *I Was a Com-*

munist for the FBI, a rather lurid, tacky, Grade-B melodrama, described as having "the form and style of gangster-syndicate films";
the production embellished, distorted, fictionalized, diluted the
Cvetic story, but it also enhanced his celebrity—and the film's subsequent continuing life as television fodder has assured Cvetic an ongoing pop fame.[6]

The courts discredited Cvetic in the mid-1950s. He had
gone too far in his testimony: a dubious reality had given way to
overexaggeration and outright mendacity. His career as a professional witness ended. But thanks to the film's continued showing on
TV he remained a hero—but as time passed, one out of context. The
anti-Communist paranoia of the early 1950s faded; the Soviet empire began to recede; new issues faced the United States domestically. However, Cvetic in a time warp continued to fight "the Red
Menace." And he did so long after many of his professional anti-
Communist colleagues (whose flame may briefly have shone more
brightly than Cvetic's at a given moment) had faded from the scene
and from memory. The REAL Cvetic did too: his death in 1962
evoked little notice. But the REEL Cvetic remained. And that film
image had allowed him to sustain himself after the mid-1950s. Some
hapless political and business ventures led him to migrate to southern California toward the end of the decade. There he joined up with
the emerging "Radical Right," which utilized his screen image. At
the time of his death in 1962 a stale, tired Cvetic—thanks to that
image—had managed to hook up with the John Birch Society and
with Billy James Hargis's Christian Crusade. Indeed his film persona
survived his death, and years later the FBI continued to receive inquiries about him from TV viewers "impressed" by the film.[7]

Cvetic and his times, especially his anti-Communist activities in Pittsburgh and its environs as well as the response to them, de-
mand attention. By chronicling and analyzing his career, the milieu
he moved in, and the issues attached to them, it is possible, in reveal-
ing sometimes surprising detail, to come to grips with the rise and
decline of zealous anti-Communism in the Pittsburgh area—and also
elsewhere to an extent. An overview of Cvetic's life and times offers
fascinating and useful insights into the creation and merchandising
of a reckless professional witness (during the breed's heyday) as well

as the distributions of his pronoucements and testimony. Especially important to note is his symbiotic relationship with various branches of government and with a media that made a hero out of him.

Thanks to media manipulation at the time of Cvetic's surfacing, never was more humble clay more engagingly and attractively molded. Unhappily for Cvetic, he frittered away his opportunities and his supporters. His fall from grace came all too quickly. Until the end, Cvetic stubbornly but vainly soldiered on in increasingly desperate attempts to mine once more the antisubversion Golconda. But he failed, and now he was, in FBI Director Hoover's apt phrase, "washed up."[8]

This book deals with how all this came to pass. Read on, and you will learn about Cvetic's life prior to his involvement with the FBI and the curious circumstances surrounding his recruitment and his break with the Bureau, as well as the various individuals involved with his surfacing. Cvetic's glory days, including the creation of the film and a radio series, are followed by the unhappy tale of his fall and death. Cvetic was not an admirable man, but he had an impact, and there is much to be learned from his story. Although not timeless, this story will have pertinence as long as the security state remains in existence and as long as people have to deal with media manipulation. Cvetic's life and adventures, his associates and detractors (many of them pure neither in motive nor in deed), make his story a cautionary tale—one to be considered carefully in light of recent developments. My aim has been, to use another historian's well-chosen words, "to explain what happened, without conscious bias in any direction."[9]

one

In the three decades before World War I broke out in 1914, tens of thousands emigrated from Slovenia, then a Balkan part of Austria-Hungary. The war ended the mass outflow. After 1918, as part of the peace settlement, Slovenia became the northwestern part of Yugoslavia and, except for a short period when Italy incorporated parts of the territory, remained so until the early 1990s when what in the 1930s had been the "Kingdom of the Serbs, Croats, and Slovenes" began to dissolve into its component parts. Between 1880 and 1914, most of the emigrants (about 250,000 people) came to the United States. The largest Slovenian colony in the United States was in Cleveland (known as "the metropolis of American Slovenes"), but a significant number settled in western Pennsylvania. Much of Cvetic's Party and FBI work centered on activities among Slovenes and other South Slav groups because of his ethnic background.[1]

Matt Cvetic's parents left what he has described as "the little Slovenian town of Vinice" and came to the United States around the turn of the century, ultimately settling in the Pittsburgh area. Did the parents, as Cvetic later claimed, find the city "an attractive fabulous land of promise," or did they like a contemporary Slovenian immigrant—the unjustly neglected writer Louis Adamic—find their ultimate destination "a vast socio-economic jungle with an ugliness . . . so honest and intense it almost becomes beauty"? Just what Cvetic's parents experienced remains unclear, given his cryptic remembrances and often contradictory testimony. Despite the prevalent nativism and racism of the Progressive era (which has led some to re-name the pre–World War I U.S. years "the regressive era"), Cvetic's father moved up from humble beginnings. He seems to have ig-nored those who castigated "the hordes" from Southern and Eastern Europe as "a very bad thing for America." The father, one of what a contemporary termed "graduates in the school of experience," scrimped and saved, bought his own home, went into business for himself, and like many of his peers operated limited family concerns that often serviced his fellow Slovenes and other South Slavs. By 1942 he owned various small properties including a service station and a building once used as a hotel.[2]

Matt Cvetic was born on March 4, 1909, in the Lawrence-ville section of Pittsburgh. Always anxious to enhance his status by any means possible, Cvetic later noted that he "was born not more than two blocks from [the] early home of . . . Stephen Foster, the beloved song writer." One of eleven children (six brothers, four sis-ters), he recalled being "a sickly child, susceptible it seemed, to every disease that came along." He finished the eighth grade at St. Mary's, a Roman Catholic grammar school, graduating at age thirteen in 1922. His formal education thereafter seems checkered and limited—just how limited remains unclear. At one 1954 court session he ini-tially answered a question about his later education at St. Vincent's (a parochial high school), "Well, I went to the prep school or college"; ultimately hostile counsel forced Cvetic to admit he had only at-tended "the ninth and tenth grades." During his initial contacts with the FBI in the early 1940s he claimed to have attended St. Vincent's for three years (a claim he often later repeated). Even during his 1950 appearance before a very friendly HUAC he fudged a bit: speaking about the completion of secretarial courses at a local business school, Cvetic testified he had "graduated from Curry Business College." During the early 1930s he rounded out his formal education with mail-order courses in "Fingerprinting, Graphology, and Cri-minal Psychology" from the Seattle-based International School of Criminology.[3]

Much of his employment record seems equally murky. Dur-ing various courtroom cross examinations, both friendly and hostile, as well as in testimony before mostly friendly congressional committees, Cvetic—in responding to questions about his employment—found it expedient as during a 1951 New York trial to respond repeatedly "I can't recall." When asked how long he may have held a specific job, he would preface his answer with "to the best of my recollection" or "about." He continually failed to reply with precision when asked about his employment or work experiences. Before becoming involved with the FBI in 1941, he had held a variety of jobs in the Pittsburgh area for varying amounts of time. In his late teens at the end of the 1920s he had a stint as a "price clerk" with a farm-implements jobber. Subsequently he worked as a sales manager for a local furniture company and as a salesman with a radio company. From 1931 to 1935 he operated service stations, either for his father or himself. For a time in the mid-1930s he worked for one of the New Deal alphabet agencies, the WPA (Works Progress Administration), as well as for other government agencies, including the Weather Bureau and the Department of Justice, for which he recalled working on a survey collating hundreds of "case histories of present and past inmates of Pennsylvania's Western Penitentiary." In December 1937 he obtained employment as a "junior" placement interviewer with the Pennsylvania Unemployment Compensation and Employment Division of the State Department of Labor and Industry, which later became part of the U.S. Employment Service.[4]

He led a tumultuous married life for much of this time. He married a pregnant eighteen-year-old Marie Dolores Barsh on August 15, 1931. The next year they had twin sons, Richard and Matt Jr. (born an unusual nine hours apart). The marriage, as he later carefully put it, "was never a happy one." His ex-wife simply felt that "as a husband he was a total failure." At one point she, Cvetic, and the children depended for food on her parents. She recalled various separations because "he was out practically every evening," gave her little on which to run the household, had "relations" with other women but not her, swore at her in front of the children and family, calling her "a cocksucker" and a "whore" among other epithets, and beat her. Cvetic seems to have regarded his wife as inferior and subservient and believed in as well as practiced such Old Country aphorisms as "he who does not beat his wife is no man."[5]

Cvetic's wife, pretty and petite, had interests such as music that escaped him: in lieu of the child support for which she at least twice unsuccessfully sued him, she earned a living as a successful piano teacher and as a church organist (nineteen years at St. Ambrose, a Pittsburgh parish). She later said that, given Cvetic's erratic record of support, without the church's job, "I would have died of hunger." Moreover, she seems to have come from a more striving family. Her sister Barbara, for example, achieved renown locally as a singer and for a time was assistant advertising manager of a monthly, *The American Slav,* the "First National Magazine of the United Slavs in America." In 1939 Cvetic's wife found it necessary to sue him for nonsupport and "monies owed." The court entered a judgment against him but suspended it when he effected a reconciliation. Neither this reconciliation nor later ones, however, proved lasting.[6]

He had real character flaws, which despite the best efforts of his enemies (especially on the Left) never did get much publicity. The hyperbolic eulogizing that surrounded him when he surfaced initially buried any negative facts about his family life. To cite just one unhappy example: in 1939 he was indicted and charged with "aggravated assault and battery" upon his sister-in-law Anna M. Barsh, a teacher. The altercation by his account resulted from an argument "concerning monies loaned him by her." During all the years various lawyers challenged his testimony they never could get him to respond fully under oath to the charges in the indictment. Cvetic would respond he "pushed Anna away," or she "just fell down," or she "slipped." In any event Anna Barsh suffered several injuries including a broken wrist, resulting in hospitalization. All this took place about 1:30 A.M., after Cvetic's wife had gone to sleep. Ultimately after what has been characterized as "much begging" on Cvetic's part, the sister-in-law agreed to a *nol pros* of the indictment in return for restitution in the amount of $340, payable in installments of $20 a month. During a fierce cross-examination at a 1951 deportation hearing, counsel repeated Anna Barsh's statement that Cvetic had thrown himself "on her shoulders and violently [thrown] her on the floor," and then attempted "a sexual attack." Cvetic responded weakly. Then as earlier the charge got only limited news-play, mostly in the far Left press. In 1950, commenting on this charge at a local Board of Election meeting just outside Pittsburgh, he asked—in words he later claimed were facetious–"When . . . was [it] a crime to beat up your sister-in-law, anyhow?" The mainstream media ignored or downplayed this comment by Cvetic–then newly anointed as an anti-Communist hero.[7]

According to a newspaperman friendly to Cvetic he had a hard time staying away from "booze and babes." By all accounts, he liked women and chased them. He later admitted that for much of his adult life he "went with more than one girl." Whatever his shortcomings, the pudgy 5 feet $4^1/_2$ inches tall Cvetic had charm and a splendidly seductive voice, which often lent credibility to the most outrageous stories. He may indeed have believed the stories he told, no matter how badly they contradicted fact or reason, when he was telling them. And this air of sincerity, at least briefly, made him a potent figure after he surfaced. Moreover, he did have imagination. In 1942, after coming to terms with the FBI, he brought two men (supposedly agents) home with him; they informed his wife that her husband would "be working for the government." After Cvetic nudged one of them and said, "Tell her of the dinners I will have . . . with women," she recalled that "they told her not to be alarmed if she heard reports that her husband was out with other women." In 1950 she remembered that they did not look like FBI agents and she wasn't inclined to believe them. By 1945 she had had enough and filed for divorce. It was granted in January 1946, with Cvetic having to pay court costs.[8]

Her story about the visit does not seem fanciful to me. But given puritanical FBI Director J. Edgar Hoover's tight rein over the Bureau, she was probably right to suspect that the "agents" were just friends of Cvetic that she didn't know. Whatever the veracity of the story, however, it does underscore the difficulty of defining clearly the beginnings of the complex relationship between Cvetic and the Bureau. Moreover, the FBI's recruitment of Cvetic needs to be placed in context. That recruitment was part of the Bureau's stepped-up prewar surveillance of "subversive activity" in the United States. Both detractors and defenders of Hoover and the Bureau agree that the origins of this escalation lie in August 1936 meetings at which President Franklin D. Roosevelt "directed" the FBI head and his agency "to develop more systematic intelligence" about

"Communist and Fascist activities" in the United States. Hoover, a master bureaucrat, built on this authorization and others he received from a president increasingly concerned about national defense, America's world role, and subversion. FDR, as one expert acknowledges, "for his own reasons welcomed the expansion of FBI surveillance activities."[9]

World War II began on September 1, 1939. Just days earlier the Soviet Union and Nazi Germany had signed the pact that gave Adolf Hitler the free hand he needed to make war. The United States would not formally enter the war until December 1941. Well before then, however, the country had begun to rearm and increasingly to assist Great Britain. After mid-1940 that country stood virtually alone against Germany—until June 22, 1941, when Hitler ended his modus vivendi with the USSR, and his legions ruthlessly waged war on it. Until the Nazi invasion American Communists—whose leadership took its marching orders from the Soviet Union—had fulminated against what they termed an "imperialistic war" and had spoken out forcefully against FDR's efforts to assist the British. The CP cry was "the Yanks are not coming." And during that period unions in which Communists held leadership positions called a number of strikes against key defense contractors such as North American Aviation and Allis Chalmers. More conservative labor leaders had castigated the Communists for calling "strikes against the government." The economist Walter Galenson is one of various scholars who point up "the Communist policy of obscuring the national defense effort . . . prior to the German invasion of Russia."[10]

Despite the visibility of the Communists the data do allow for a less baleful review of their actions. Nineteen forty-one was a banner year for strikes, many by unions far removed from Communism: one history records that "the number of American Labor disputes in 1941 reached a higher total than in any previous year, with the single exception of 1937." But in 1941 what has been dubbed "the hysteria of the time" even affected a harried President Roosevelt. His usual sangfroid masked deep concerns. Hoover, ever since war's outbreak in 1939, had expanded the Bureau's range of "antisubversive" activity. The brouhaha over CP influence, coupled with FDR's concerns, allowed Hoover to give play to what a former agent termed the Director's "passionate crusade against Communism." It was in this atmosphere that Cvetic and the FBI came into contact. Both before and after the invasion of the USSR, the FBI increasingly infiltrated the American Communist Party, an initiative that was to benefit Cvetic a great deal.[11]

The FBI, in order to effect that infiltration, recruited all kinds of people in different parts of the country and significantly broadened its confidential informant program. These FBI plants in the Party would only surface years later as needed in court and congressional hearings. Their testimony there and subsequently in other venues such as deportation hearings remained unimpeachable until well into the 1950s. Then, as with Cvetic, a significant number of the plants were found unreliable. But initially, as more than one observer noted, the testimony of the informants disoriented and demoralized the Party's leadership. This was especially true after Herbert Philbrick, Angela Calomiris, and others had testified in the first of the Smith Act prosecutions at the end of the 1940s; many of these informants had been recruited earlier in the decade as part of Hoover's program of expansion.[12]

The Massachusetts-based Philbrick began his stint as a self-styled "counterspy" in 1941. Angela Calomiris recalled being visited in her Greenwich Village apartment and photo studio in early 1942 by agents inviting her "to join the Communist Party and observe for the FBI." The Bureau recruited in western Pennsylvania as well. In the Pittsburgh area George Dietze and Joseph Mazzei, both named as Communists by Cvetic during his initial 1950 HUAC appearance, later proved to have begun working for the FBI in 1940 and 1941 respectively.[13]

Cvetic always insisted that it was his unsuccessful attempt to join Army Intelligence in 1939 that had brought him to the attention of the Bureau. He remembered claiming on that application, as he would subsequently after surfacing, command of seven East European languages (Slovenian, Croatian, Serbian, Lithuanian, Russian, Slovak, and Polish). He attributed his rejection, not to educational shortcomings or to limited job experience, but to "physical reasons." That could well have been so. The short, overweight Cvetic had suffered from recurrent bouts of ill health and during the mid-1930s needed some psychiatric care for what years later his ex-wife described as "big ideas, big imagination." Then and periodically thereafter he was a patient of Dr. H. L. Mitchell, who in 1950 was head of the University of Pittsburgh's Department of Psychiatry, and a head of staff at St. Francis Hospital. Mitchell described Cvetic as "the victim of a firmly fixed 'anxiety neurosis' being of the unjustifiable conviction that he suffered from heart disease." Neither these shortcomings nor Cvetic's disturbed personal life seems to have disqualified him in the eyes of the Pittsburgh FBI, understandably anxious to carry out Hoover's orders to find informants who would report on the presumed infiltration of the CP into the Pittsburgh area's ethnic communities.[14]

Cvetic recalled nearly a decade later that two FBI agents approached him in April 1941, months after his putative rejection by the Army. They expressed concern about Communist-inspired strikes hampering the national interest, and about "Reds" at the employment service "who could exert a tremendous influence over . . . policies and personnel." And just as the New York agents had reached out to Calomiris, the Pittsburgh agents asked Cvetic (to use his words) if he would keep "an eye open for Communists." He quickly agreed to do so and, as the FBI files make clear, over the next months provided information on what a Bureau report tersely called "the alleged Communist element."[15]

Cvetic met about once a month with his "FBI advisers" (as he dubbed them). At their behest he "curried the Reds' favor" while reporting on them. He attended meetings and rallies as well as other functions large and small, bought Communist books and periodicals, assisted Party members in finding certain kinds of jobs insofar as his employment service position allowed, and spoke out vigorously in support of CP causes at work and elsewhere. By the end of 1942 the Pittsburgh Communist leadership accepted that he was (in his words) "good material." In February 1943 he achieved his goal of becoming a member of the Communist Party. Just exactly how that took place remains open to question (as does so much of Cvetic's early career). His HUAC testimony, later writings, and an FBI report all agree that on a given February day he joined the Party. But to consider just one *question* about that enrollment, how did CP National Board member Elizabeth Gurley Flynn fit into that particular day: Rashōmonlike each source has a different answer, for example, about why she came to speak in Pittsburgh.[16]

As a member of the Communist Party, Cvetic continued to attend meetings, often two or three evenings a week; he continued through the employment service to help Communists and their friends find jobs to which access would have been more difficult otherwise; he continued to sell the CP newspaper the *Daily Worker*. He went to "Red propaganda movies," participated in classes at a "Marxist Leninist school," took an active part in CP membership recruitment drives, and helped organize and lead "education discussions" at the various branches of the Pittsburgh-area CP to which he belonged. He became active in "nationality work," joining Slovenian and other Slav fraternal organizations which he (and others) tried "to change into Party fronts." He picketed and marched on behalf of various Communist causes in Pittsburgh and elsewhere, and held some minor official positions on various local CP committees. Indeed he proved such a militant that the Bureau asked him "to be more discreet in his Communist Party activities," and in December 1944 called off a public investigation of Communists at the employment service in Pittsburgh "in order to take suspicion off Cvetic because his more conservative colleagues found it strange" the FBI had not interviewed him along with other suspected Reds. A concerned Hoover urged the Pittsburgh FBI to "carefully supervise Cvetic's public activities."[17]

Cvetic claimed that during the seven years he belonged to the Communist Party, "the reports I made to the FBI totaled 20,000 typewritten pages." Even though by my count that comes to approximately fifty-nine pages a week, Cvetic may well not have exaggerated much. He turned in a thirty-three-page "typewritten report" on just one 1945 Cleveland meeting. And his reports "from 4/1/45 to 2/3/49" resulted in "twelve bound volumes." He often used the cover name Bob Lee in reports "just in case." In addition to his reports, declared Cvetic after surfacing, he had supplied the FBI with "30,000 pages of exhibits, letters, press releases, pamphlets and other propaganda publications" and he had "reported the names of about 1,000 Communist Party members, the majority living in Western

Pennsylvania . . . but also in Chicago, Cleveland, New York City, and Washington D.C." He also performed other tasks for the FBI, such as identifying individuals who had been surreptitiously filmed entering or leaving Party meetings. The Bureau (to use Cvetic's words) "covered the more important meetings like a blanket," and he attended screenings held at the FBI's offices where he identified whomever he could.[18]

Although occasionally erratic, in the main Cvetic served the FBI diligently. However one may ultimately estimate the quality of his reports to the Bureau, it considered him extremely useful for much of his tenure as a confidential informant. Special Agents in Charge (SACs) of the FBI's Pittsburgh office reported to Hoover on Cvetic's "excellent results," praised his "detailed reports on Party plans, policies, and personnel," and described him as "a most valuable source." The Pittsburgh agents believed that Cvetic provided the Bureau with hard-to-obtain information "on general Communist activities in the foreign language field." Hoover, not necessarily blinded by his passionate anti-Communism, at one point after reviewing Cvetic's record, referred to him as "the best possibility that the Bureau has to get into the inner circle of the Communist Party." In 1949, notwithstanding Cvetic's deteriorating relationship with the FBI and the ensuing problems, Hoover continued to emphasize the informant's "inestimable value to the Bureau's work." And even after Cvetic surfaced in February 1950, despite intense FBI dissatisfaction both with how that took place and with his HUAC appearance, a Bureau appraisal lauded him as "one of the most productive informants we have had."[19]

Not too long after he surfaced Cvetic began to refer to the perils he had faced because of his undercover work. He did so with increasing frequency as the decade wore on and he slipped from the headlines. In his imaginative 1959 memoir, privately printed just a few years before his death, Cvetic argued that exposure of his ties to the Bureau could have had serious consequences: Not only would his "usefulness to the FBI have ended" but he would have also faced "the threat of savage Communist reprisal . . . , brainwashing, torture or even death." Melodramatically, Cvetic described one situation where it seemed he had been found out as "a leak to the FBI," and (to use his words) "I was in for a good going over by the Commie goon squad." But in this instance, as in others, he worried unnecessarily. The history of Communism and the Party in the United States, as elsewhere in the world, has its (too often unsubstantiated) share of mysterious "suicides," unexplained disappearances, and dubious political murders—but Cvetic discovered dangers to himself only after he had become stale news, the public had lost interest in him, and most of the professional anti-Communists had discarded him. When Cvetic surfaced in 1950, "being tossed out of the Party" was the only risk he mentioned.[20]

After he surfaced, Cvetic also said, "One of the prices I had to pay for doing the work I did was having my family think me a jerk, maybe even a traitor." He strongly implied that the demands made on him in maintaining a façade as a dedicated Communist disturbed his private life and that of his family. Rather disingenuously he blamed the undercover work for his 1946 divorce and for prolonged separation from his sons. He maintained that they were "badgered" in school by other children who resented the sons' portrayal of their father's seemingly zealous Communist activities. He maintained that his efforts for the FBI resulted in difficult relationships with his brothers and sisters, who (Cvetic remembered) made it clear that he "wasn't welcome in their homes." He claimed especially to regret that his mother died in ignorance of his FBI connection (a situation played up by the media with such tag lines as that in the *Pittsburgh Press,* "Mother died thinking he was a Communist"). Over and over again he recalled for the media that just two weeks before her death in 1949 she was still "begging me to change my name so I wouldn't humiliate the rest of the Cvetics." He felt that "I couldn't tell her about my real job," because she "might have given me away without meaning to do so."[21]

Cvetic later maintained that this undercover status also prevented him from finding any solace in his religion: "If it had got around that I was still a Catholic, my sincerity as a Communist would have been suspect." Later he remembered that his sons "ragged" him for missing Mass. Cvetic remembered that, even at his beloved mother's funeral, because Communist friends and coworkers attended, he had to "keep up my act" and "kick about there being so much sanctimonious stuff." Months later it still saddened him that two of his brothers had supposedly wanted "to take me outside and beat my brains out but my father persuaded them not to." In another version of this story, Cvetic asserted that "my oldest brother, who was calmer, talked them out of it." [22]

These images of sacrifice, suffering, and dedication (themes typical of the stories told by most FBI plants after they surfaced) were highlights of his 1950 HUAC testimony, the initial media coverage, a feature film, and his subsequent public appearances. These images in the main had no more grounding in reality than did the perils an opportunistic Cvetic claimed to have faced. Far from attacking him for being a Communist, the Cvetic family as one sister said in 1950, "kidded him about being a Communist and laughed at him." Another of Cvetic's sisters, said at that time, "We didn't turn against him because after all he was our own flesh and blood." His sister Hildegarde, a devout Catholic nun, said she never had stopped "praying" for her brother. His sons, who believed he "loved our country dearly," understood that it was not FBI work that had marred their family life. In 1950 Matt Junior said that because of separations and the divorce he "never got to know" his father "very well." Years later Richard described him as "a weak husband" and a "weak father." [23]

Patriotism might well have prompted Cvetic's decision initially to become an FBI informant. But Cvetic's brother Ben later recalled that "Matty always liked intrigue." Certainly, money played no role at first, for the agents who initially contacted Cvetic in 1941 had informed him that he would be operating on a "voluntary no-pay basis." After his formal enrollment in the Party in February 1943 Cvetic informed the Pittsburgh FBI that in his estimation he had spent more than $200 in pursuit of Party membership (taking out subscriptions, buying literature, contributing to various causes). The agents, surprised but pleased that Cvetic had asked "for no remuneration whatever," recommended to Hoover that he receive $15 a week "compensation," which should serve to cover his costs as a Party member. Hoover agreed.[24]

Shortly after Cvetic received his first payments, the Bureau informed him that "he may expect increases in the compensation . . .

afforded . . . in accordance with the value of [his] information." The Bureau obviously valued Cvetic's efforts, for by the end of 1943 the FBI was already paying him $35 weekly. Within less than two years the weekly stipend rose to $50. This had increased to $65 by 1947. The next year the Bureau raised the payment to $85, a handsome weekly salary for 1948. Supposedly $20 of that sum was for expenses, but Cvetic strongly objected to accounting for those funds and generally failed to do so. Soon the Bureau waived the requirement. Moreover, during all Cvetic's years as an informant, the Bureau supplemented the weekly stipend by paying many of the expenses he incurred as a result of his anti-Communist activity (dues, subscriptions, telephone calls, assessments by the Party and front organizations). The Bureau, for example, reimbursed Cvetic when the Party did not for expenditures such as $99.77 laid out for taxi fares and "entertainment" while attending a 1945 front organization convention in Cleveland.[25]

It would seem that the FBI payments Cvetic received meant more than he ever publicly admitted. In December 1945 he resigned from his employment service position; he always maintained that he had been forced out by his strongly anti-Communist supervisor ("You quit or you're fired—Civil Service or not"). At the time he resigned Cvetic was earning little more from that job than he was receiving from the FBI. As it was, for more than half of his eight-year tenure with the employment service he was earning less than $40 a week. Moreover, the Bureau paid him in cash, and later under oath, he admitted that he hadn't reported the income on his tax returns for those years. It seems that he never paid any taxes on his FBI earnings. His rationale being, Cvetic some years later asserted, that "it would have been too risky—for a disloyal clerk, or a simple blabbermouth, could have spilled the beans."[26]

A certain intriguing murky quality to his finances and his employment marks the next few years of Cvetic's life. During at least part of 1946 he worked for the Communist-controlled American Committee for Yugoslav Relief (later claiming it paid him the equivalent of his $60 a week FBI stipend). This double-dipping continued in the first part of 1947 as he worked for the Communist-dominated American Slav Congress as executive secretary of its important western Pennsylvania branch, until supposedly forced to step aside for a "more important comrade." Thereafter he had brief paid stints with some front groups such as Pittsburgh's Labor Press Committee (created to raise funds for Communist publications). He also earned a salary briefly as part of the Communist infusion into the Progressive Party (a Left-leaning organization which in a committed but inadequate campaign ran the then-friendly-to-the-Soviets Henry Wallace for president in 1948). To quell any Party suspicions about his sources of income, Cvetic later said that he told the Party that he was working at some menial job or another, such as a carpenter's helper or as a package wrapper at Kaufmann's (a Pittsburgh department store). He declared under oath in various court proceedings that he had faked such "cover jobs"; however, some Bureau people believed that he actually worked these jobs or similar ones but later was embarrassed, given his celebrity, to admit such inconsequential employment. In any event if he had such employment he certainly neglected to inform the FBI, and if he had any income beyond his FBI weekly payments, he badly needed it.[27]

After the presidential election in November 1948 until he surfaced in February 1950, Cvetic—to maintain his "cover" and supposedly to supplement his Bureau pay—sold insurance on a commission basis for an agency run by a friend. Cvetic did obtain state licenses as an agent for various life insurance and casualty companies in December 1948. He later claimed to have sold many policies, especially to "my Communist friends." He supposedly insured Western Pennsylvania CP leader Steve Nelson's automobile, a claim Nelson very angrily denied. Cvetic may have done as well selling insurance as he later claimed, but at least one Pittsburgh FBI agent believed he had done "nil." Cvetic constantly complained to the local Bureau about being debt ridden and needing more money. He repeatedly demanded an increase in his stipend to $100 a week, so much so that the Pittsburgh FBI queried Hoover about how to respond to Cvetic's "insatiable desire for salary increases." The Pittsburgh agents, rightly or wrongly, valued Cvetic's efforts but did not have to read between the lines when Hoover commented that "there are not many informants . . . being paid a sum as high as Cvetic." During 1949 Cvetic continued to demand a raise to $100 a week and threatened to quit if he did not get it.[28]

For many of his undercover years Cvetic, as a result of his family problems, commuted between a series of furnished rooms and his parents' home. Finally in 1945 he settled in a room at the William Penn, the largest and one of the finest hotels in Pittsburgh. The hotel had other interesting long-term occupants, among them the labor racketeer Nick Stirone, who resided in a luxurious suite when not at his 742-acre farm. Cvetic had decided on hotel living, he said, because it would facilitate his undercover work ("My FBI contacts could drop in . . . with less chance of being noticed"). He lived under the pseudonym Bob Stanton, the name being derived from his FBI *nom de plume* (Bob Lee) and the address of his parents, who lived on Stanton Avenue.[29]

Cvetic maintained he had made a "deal" with the Statler-managed hotel to pay for the room on a monthly basis, which kept the cost ($105) within what he could afford. Steve Nelson has charged that Cvetic lived there "gratis" in return for "stooling" on the activities of the Pittsburgh local of the hotel and restaurant workers' union. There may be some validity to this charge: Cvetic later claimed that his sworn testimony about Communists in the Pittsburgh local had resulted in its members voting to give "the Reds . . . the old heave-ho." The writer David Caute has pointed out that among the many Cvetic "fingered" were two leaders of the hotel and restaurant workers' local, who given the option to deny Cvetic's charges or to resign, chose to resign.[30]

After Cvetic surfaced, the William Penn's general manager described "how he helped Matt . . . for the past five years . . . moving his room around the hotel from floor to floor for fear somebody might be on his trail." That no one was on that trail for much of that time was surprising. Cvetic did not keep his undercover work as deep a secret as he later claimed. He blabbed to others besides the hotel manager. Cvetic had taken Father Daniel Lawless, the vigorous leader of a downtown Pittsburgh church into his confidence, and Lawless granted him, said Cvetic, a "special dispensation to give up attending Mass and receiving the sacraments" (so no Communist would catch him practicing his religion). Monsignor Rice recalls

Cvetic talking about his FBI ties not solely with priests like Father Lawless and himself, hinting strongly about those ties in unlikely public places—even in "Paddy's Horse Room, a well-known downtown Pittsburgh betting parlor frequented by many of the city's newspapermen." A Hearst reporter James Moore, through what he euphemistically termed "a set of unusual circumstances" (they both frequented the same bars and betting parlors), discovered in 1946 that the FBI employed Cvetic. By then as Cvetic later admitted he had also revealed his "connections with the FBI to his eldest brother, his psychiatrist," and "to more than one girl."[31]

In 1947, as the result of a bizarre series of events, the Pittsburgh FBI became formally aware of Cvetic's indiscretions. At the time Cvetic was in pursuit of a woman he later referred to as "Helen Newman," a Stouffer's Restaurant cashier in her late twenties whom he hoped to marry. The father—on learning of Cvetic's Communist affiliations—supposedly told him "we don't want any God-damned Communist in this house. . . . If I ever see you around here again I'll blow your head off." The mother became so agitated about Cvetic wooing her daughter that she had "fainting spells, fits, and attacks of blindness" when his name was mentioned. How serious the relationship was between Cvetic and "Helen" remains unclear. He fondly remembered giving her a cocker spaniel that they walked together. When she became engaged to another man, Cvetic told her about his FBI ties. She told her parents but did not break off her engagement. Cvetic, anxious to have his story confirmed, asked his Bureau contacts to talk with the woman and her parents. The Pittsburgh FBI, dismayed at this breach of security, "forcefully advised" Cvetic that the Bureau would not contact the woman or her parents.[32]

Hoover and the Pittsburgh office considered discontinuing Cvetic as a confidential informant as a result of this blatant indiscretion. But because his services were considered "extremely reliable," Hoover decided to keep him on. Always fond of the bottle, Cvetic may have been "under the influence" when he disclosed his ties to "Helen Newman" and her parents. And for the FBI worse was to come. One morning in the latter part of 1947, after a night out, he regained consciousness in the city jail and later maintained that "someone slipped me a Mickey Finn." According to one account, on being arrested for drunk and disorderly conduct he had shouted out "you can't do this to me, I work for the FBI." In that instance Cvetic may have been caught up in a temporary crackdown on "private drinking clubs," occasioned by political pressure (one of the police raiders said they had acted because "the heat's on").[33]

Despite the stream of hyperbolic prose poured out by the media in Pittsburgh and elsewhere when Cvetic surfaced that he was "one of Pittsburgh's top Communists," and despite his subsequent much-repeated self-aggrandizing claim about being "Nelson's lieutenant and right-hand man," Cvetic never was a "big gun" or "one of the Party leaders in western Pennsylvania" (to use just two of the newspapers' favorite phrases). On the contrary Cvetic never rose above the Party's lower echelons. A detailed 1949 HUAC report on the American Slav Congress, for example, mentions various office-holders and other persons many times but refers to Cvetic only in passing as a "Slovenian Communist Party member."[34]

The Communists, perhaps because they moved in different circles, do not seem to have found out about Cvetic's ties with the FBI until perhaps late in the day. In 1950, soon after Cvetic surfaced, various CP leaders asserted that they had begun to suspect he was an informant and for some time; Nelson said he had known for "the past six months that Cvetic had been working for the FBI." Nelson, who came to "despise" Cvetic, denigrated him as "Pittsburgh's Number 1 informer—a mental mediocrity" who "lied and slandered." Nelson later asserted that "Cvetic knew . . . we were . . . aware that there was something fishy about him." Given Cvetic's many indiscretions, he may well have blown his cover, and Nelson's and the Party's assertions may well be true by the end of 1949, but earlier that was certainly not the case. Cvetic himself later said that toward the end of his Communist career he was "merely doing odd jobs for the Party." Yet Cvetic, until he surfaced, continued attending Party meetings. And he seems to have been trusted enough that at the last moment he could make off with some eighty pounds of Party and front organizations "bank statements, check stub books, minute books of meetings, radio scripts, letters, credentials, and accounting statements" (all of which he turned over to HUAC just before his initial appearance before the Committee). And notwithstanding the statements of

Nelson and other CP officials after the fact, the Pittsburgh FBI, which had a variety of pipelines into the Party in Pittsburgh and elsewhere, as late as the end of November 1949 did not believe that Cvetic had been "made." [35]

Actually, whether he had been found out or not made little difference. Cvetic had so to speak run out of gas. The rapidly changing public attitude toward Communism after World War II had made him uneasy. Cvetic joined the Party in 1943 at the height of the war, when in Pittsburgh as elsewhere in the United States, red-baiting had virtually ceased. Communism was an integral part of the war effort, and the Soviet Union was a "valiant" ally. After 1945, the Soviet Union became "the enemy" and the Cold War intensified. In heavily Catholic Pittsburgh the repression of the Church in Eastern Europe by Soviet-initiated Communist regimes engendered an especially emotional response. Anxiety soon turned into overt hostility as American Catholic leaders in defense of their religion denounced "Christ-baiting Communists . . . men who as their God know only Satan and Stalin," and charged that these "satanic Soviet sycophants" in the United States "would betray their country to a godless and inhuman ideology." [36]

It was then that Cvetic, because of his Communist ties, probably began to face some of the problems in Pittsburgh with family and friends so played up by the media in 1950. Communism for many, as the *Reader's Digest* put it, had become a "menace to freedom." The issue, as was later noted, became "clear cut": there existed right and wrong, good and evil—all "without compromise or doubt." Communists, those suspected of being Communists, or those judged to be following the Party line faced real ostracism, loss of employment, and economic discrimination (such as denial of jobs). In 1947, as Nelson recalled, the Party had sponsored a meeting in downtown Pittsburgh, and some seven hundred people had assembled to hear Party leaders "speak without incident." But soon mob violence began to engulf Communist meetings. Cvetic faced real physical dangers but not from his "comrades." [37]

In April 1949, in a preview of the hysteria that would soon dominate much of Pittsburgh life, hundreds of demonstrators mobbed the approximately three hundred people leaving a meeting billed as "a protest against the trial of 11 top Communists in New York." Barely half the hall had been filled for the meeting, and the limited attendance disappointed the organizers, recalled Cvetic, who was on the arrangements committee. At the meeting's end, the participants faced as they left what Nelson described as "a concerted attack." The demonstrators, as one newsman reported, "mussed up men and women alike, pummeling some with fists." Some of the attendees who had managed to escape the mob and gotten into a taxi were ordered by the driver to get out: "I'm not hauling Commies." Cvetic later complained, "We were hit by pop bottles, our clothes fouled by spittle, and we were shoved around."[38]

Cvetic suddenly found himself in an unexpected dilemma. His Communist links, while still lucrative per se because of his FBI undercover work, were causing him distress. Never emotionally strong, or the most stable of individuals, Cvetic could not cope with his situation. The FBI agents who met with him categorized Cvetic as increasingly "moody . . . subject to alternating periods of enthusiasm, self-pity, and depression." The Bureau always had pegged him as "a neurotic personality." Cvetic later claimed that months earlier he had wanted to cut and run, to extricate himself from what he termed his "double life." However, there seems to be no evidence to substantiate this wish other than his later comments.[39]

He did press the FBI in 1949 to let "the world" know about his undercover work. But the Bureau refused to disclose the job "I'd been doing and thereby re-establish me as a loyal citizen." Notwithstanding recommendations made by Pittsburgh and Washington FBI officials, a recalcitrant Hoover felt going public would be bad policy and decided that, as in "all such cases, no press release of any kind will be made by the Bureau regarding him." Hoover further determined that if Cvetic attempted to capitalize on his FBI ties, the Bureau should make no comment and so instructed the Pittsburgh office. The Director could not anticipate what ultimately took place.[40]

As a result of the "Helen Newman" contretemps the Bureau had considered "discontinuing" its ties with Cvetic, but had not done so because of his seeming value as a source and more important because of a belief in his potential as a pipeline into CP activities nationally. That potential seemed realizable if Cvetic accepted an anticipated transfer to New York City by the Party. Whether the call would have come or not is open to question but Hoover felt Cvetic was "procrastinating." The Pittsburgh FBI agents who dealt with Cvetic believed that the prospect of moving to New York City "did not appeal to him," that he was unwilling to leave Pittsburgh.[41]

Cvetic later indicated that he was no longer interested in working as an informant; he wanted out. He actually stood a good chance of getting the boot. Further indiscretions by him about his FBI ties had come to the attention of the Pittsburgh Bureau. In looking for a job in late 1948 he had discussed his FBI ties with a steel company executive. On December 23, 1948, the concerned head of the Pittsburgh FBI recommended to Hoover the "immediate discontinuance" of Cvetic. Hoover's staff agreed with this recommendation, but "to get back some of our investment . . . , to get as much out of him as we can," they advocated using Cvetic as a government witness in the Smith Act prosecutions of the CP national leadership.[42]

That 1940 act—formally titled "An Alien Registration Act"—was the first peacetime federal sedition law since 1798. It was popularly named after its prime mover, the conservative congressman Howard Smith, a Democrat from rural Virginia. A key provision of the act made it a crime "to conspire to teach, advocate, or encourage the overthrow" of the U.S. government. The Justice Department first obtained indictments of Communists under the act in mid-1948, and well into the 1950s prosecuted CP leaders under its provisions for conspiring to advocate the forceful overthrow of the U.S. government. Philbrick, the first FBI plant to surface and a man ultimately much envied by Cvetic, was a key witness in the first Smith Act prosecutions. He wrote (apparently with the help of the Bureau) a bestselling account of his experiences as "Comrade Herb" while working for the FBI.[43]

Hoover accepted this suggestion of using Cvetic as a witness in the initial Smith Act prosecution. Cvetic, delighted that his FBI ties would become public under what seemed to him very favorable circumstances, agreed to testify—provided that the government made clear that he was an "undercover agent" and not a "stool pigeon who . . . sold out." The prosecution agreed. The FBI made

Cvetic available to the government's attorneys. The marathon trial
had already begun when in February 1949 Cvetic went to New York
City to be interviewed by these attorneys (the trial, which had begun
in January, lasted into October 1949). Initially he was known as Paul
Sloan to the prosecutors, who "privately advised" the FBI that "the
informant would make a good government witness," but wanted to
review his reports and personal life. Subsequently, an assistant to the
Attorney General flew to Pittsburgh and spent three days interviewing Cvetic. The Bureau continued to believe that Cvetic "might be of
value in connection with the current Communist Party trial in New
York City" so the question of "discontinuance" did not seriously
arise for a while. The prosecution ultimately did not use Cvetic at the
trial because "the U.S. Attorney limited his witnesses." [44]

That decision "was a bitter disappointment," recalled
Cvetic, who said he "felt as if somebody had kicked me in the belly."
From then on he increasingly "kept at the FBI" in seemingly contradictory fashion, not only to raise his stipend but also to acknowledge
his undercover work and to help him find "another government job"
(he complained to the Pittsburgh FBI that "the nature of [his] work"
had caused him to lose his "Civil Service status"). Although he still
felt "comfortable" with the Bureau, it (both in Pittsburgh and Washington) discussed his "discontinuance." He remained "unaware of
his . . . status with the Bureau" (as one agent reported). [45]

The Pittsburgh FBI wanted to discontinue Cvetic as soon as
possible. Hoover concurred. The delay in firing Cvetic resulted not
from any consideration for him but a fear on every level of the FBI
privy to the situation that "he might be the source of some embarrassment to the Bureau." Some on Hoover's staff suggested advising
the Immigration and Naturalization Service (INS) about Cvetic's potential as a witness. They argued that this would give Cvetic the public acknowledgment he desired, *and* that "it can be pointed out to
him that his services are no longer available in view of his public dis-
closure and he can be told further payments cannot be made to
him." The idea of becoming what one FBI bureaucrat described as a
"professional witness for INS" appealed to Cvetic, but nothing came
of the idea at the time because Cvetic's circumstances changed dramatically. [46]

Cvetic still tried to get the FBI to raise his stipend, threatening to resign if not paid more and simultaneously asking for severance pay. An annoyed Hoover frowned on that possibility, deeming "the establishment of such a precedent . . . undesirable if not illegal." In November 1949 Cvetic momentarily backtracked, saying the Bureau had "misinterpreted" him. Amazingly, despite all the Bureau's problems with Cvetic, it–at the end of November–renewed his informant status and pay for another six months. Within days the Pittsburgh FBI learned that Cvetic in looking for a way to capitalize on his Bureau ties had told several more people about them over a period of weeks. The FBI fired Cvetic effective January 3, 1950, although agreeing to pay him through January 23. Hoover made it clear to the Pittsburgh office that "no consideration is to be given to any possible future use of the informant by the Bureau," and in turn Pittsburgh agents on January 23, 1950 "specifically advised" Cvetic that "no further contacts . . . would be sought."[47]

The FBI's firing of Cvetic, insofar as I can ascertain, never came to light until I discussed it in my article on him published in 1991. No hint of the dumping had ever been articulated publicly. Such politically disparate individuals as Steve Nelson and Monsignor Rice expressed surprise when I discussed with them the FBI's dumping of Cvetic: Arthur Sabin's splendid monograph on the 1951 New York trial resulting in the liquidation of the International Workers Order was in manuscript when my article appeared. Cvetic at this trial was utilized in Sabin's phrase as an "anti-Communist 'star' performer." I recall that after reading my article Sabin added a paragraph before publication about "salient facts" hitherto not known. At the time Cvetic surfaced the story was simply that Cvetic and the FBI had come to a parting of the ways. The *Pittsburgh Post-Gazette,* for example, said the relationship had ended by "mutual agreement." And phrases like that then and subsequently stood as an unchallenged explanation, especially in the absence of any official FBI comment in 1950 or later.[48]

Over the years Cvetic managed to fool even the most tenacious attorneys about the end of his relationship with the Bureau. The Pittsburgh lawyer Hyman Schlesinger, who confronted Cvetic in court and at INS hearings many times, dug up a great deal of information on a man he loathed. Some of it was not sustainable, such as reports about a "hotel credit card utilized for purposes of promiscuity," but for all Schlesinger's digging I found nothing in his files which indicated that he ever suspected that Cvetic had been fired. If he had known about it, Schlesinger certainly would have used that information as he used other knowledge gained about Cvetic's life to discredit him as a witness.[49]

Even under the most strenuous cross-examination Cvetic seems never to have slipped, although during his turn at the International Workers Order (IWO) decertification trial the organization's attorneys flustered Cvetic numerous times. Repeatedly in response to their questions Cvetic responded, "I don't recall," "I do not remember," and at one point when queried about his HUAC testimony a year earlier, "I don't recall what I testified there." Yet the IWO attorneys for all their attack on Cvetic did not consider it necessary to follow up his statement that the relationship with the FBI ended by "mutual consent."[50]

Cvetic accepted his dismissal by the FBI with seeming equanimity, telling the Pittsburgh agents who brought him the news that he did not "hold any ill will toward the Bureau." On previous occasions when Cvetic had been faced with "discontinuance" (because of his indiscretions) he had been much more emotional. He had blustered, carried on nervously, and given way to "weeping." This time the loss of his main source of income since 1947 did not seem to upset him. In the FBI agents' multipage report on this meeting Cvetic is said a number of times to have talked of "selling" his story. And his equanimity stemmed from the fact that he had done just that. The Pittsburgh individuals with whom, as the Bureau noted, he had recently discussed his FBI ties had made arrangements for him to appear before HUAC as a witness and otherwise to cash in on his years of undercover work. They promised to help him capitalize on it financially, and politically.[51]

And so they did. He was thrown more than a lifeline. For a few years thereafter Cvetic, a little man not just in height, had the power to ruin people's lives and to command respect he did not deserve. It is worthwhile detailing his career before he burst onto the public scene because it is the unlikely foundation on which was built a short-lived career of lies, exaggerations, and distortions which spread "like measles among the Aztecs" (to use historian J. H. Plumb's apt simile).[52]

two

The Background

The individuals who enabled Cvetic to surface before HUAC expected to benefit from the exposure of his FBI work in a variety of
ways. Cash certainly motivated some of them, as it motivated Cvetic.
But all those involved with Cvetic's outing held anti-Communist beliefs of some intensity. However they had come by such beliefs, all
these individuals had contributed to what might be called "prema-
ture" anti-Communism, a foretaste of the virulence that (to a greater
extent than in most parts of the United States) would engulf western
Pennsylvania. That region's newspapers, which in 1950 gave such a
favorable play to Cvetic on his surfacing, evidence this precocious
red-baiting. Consider their response, eighteen months earlier, to the
Progressive Party's attempt to get on the 1948 presidential ballot in
Pennsylvania. The *Pittsburgh Sun-Telegraph* editorialized about "Communists, Henry Wallace, and 'Progressives.' " Area newspapers, including the *Pittsburgh Press* and the *York Dispatch,* undertook what the
writer Karl Schmidt characterized as "an unconventional contribu-
tion to public information": the papers, as part of their equating Progressives and Communists, published on their front pages lists giving
the names, addresses, and occupations of those who had signed
the petitions to place the Progressive Party (and thus Wallace) on the
ballot.[1]

This attempt at intimidation aroused not only controversy
but also condemnation. As might be expected, the American Civil
Liberties Union protested vigorously, but so did many Pennsylvani-

ans. The *Press* reported a "flood" of letters—the "majority" of which opposed its actions. And despite the pressures that resulted from being listed, few of the petition signers found it necessary to recant. Progressives from all over the United States met in a national convention in Philadelphia during mid-July 1948, and nominated Wallace as their candidate for the presidency. Communists did play a significant role in his subsequent electoral campaign, just as they had in organizing the Progressive Party. However, for all their dedication and effectiveness, even scholars friendly to the Communist effort agree, as historian Richard Walton points out, that "their participation was an albatross around Wallace's neck."[2]

The weight of that albatross increased geometrically over the next months. In February 1950 the Pittsburgh papers again published the names and addresses of the dozens of area residents mentioned by Cvetic in his testimony before HUAC that month. And in the main, the press escaped criticism. The playwright Arthur Miller has marvelously summarized the change in public attitude: "A point arrived . . . when the rules of social intercourse quite suddenly changed . . . , and attitudes . . . were now made unholy, morally repulsive, . . . if not actually treasonous." Despite the thin soil in which it grew, the Communist issue had come to the forefront of American life. Events at home and abroad in the late 1940s led to a state of affairs that at least temporarily made it possible for Cvetic to function as a professional anti-Communist.[3]

The draconian Soviet clampdown on Eastern Europe in 1947 and 1948, along with the February 1948 Communist coup in Czechoslovakia, disturbed many Americans, but especially stirred the East European ethnic communities in western Pennsylvania. Pittsburgh had a large Polish population. Many among it were bitterly anti-Communist. This attitude is understandable given the Soviet Union's track record in Poland: the 1939 Nazi-Soviet Pact allowing Germany to invade Poland, the Soviet annexation at World War II's end of eastern Poland, the murder in Katyn Forest and elsewhere of thousands of Polish officers (as one history puts it "ordered by Stalin and carried out by the NKVD"—the Soviet secret police), the breaking of the Russian promise made at the 1945 Yalta conference to President Roosevelt of free elections in postwar Poland (promulgated in the conference's joint "Declaration on Liberated Europe"), and the arrest of thousands of anti-Communist Poles in 1945–46. Also Pittsburgh had its share of Polish veterans who had fought on the Allied side during World War II; nominally on the winning side, the hostility of the newly established Communist government in Poland meant exile—the bitterness among these men and their families was staggering.[4]

The split in mid-1948 between the Soviet Union and Yugoslavia also affected many in those western Pennsylvania communities. The break was between brands of Communism, but Yugoslavia chose a much more nationalist course, and as Cvetic later recounted, the Soviet Union's adherents in the ethnic communities fought to retain control of various front groups. Naturally, the more conservative ethnics continued to oppose Yugoslavia's brand of Communism as well. Russian activity elsewhere in the world also shook up Americans, who felt threatened by such events as the 321-day blockade of West Berlin instituted by the Soviets in mid-1948, and the "loss" of China at the end of 1949 when the long running civil war there ended in a Communist victory. In February 3, 1950—just days before Cvetic's HUAC appearance, and not long after the U.S. atomic monopoly had been successfully challenged by the USSR—news stories revealed that the Soviets had successfully infiltrated a spy into American atomic installations during World War II. Physicist Klaus Fuchs, a refugee from Nazi Germany who had found asylum in England, admitted that while "working in the closed circle of Anglo-American atomic secrets" he had passed on information to the Soviets.[5]

The media sensationalized Fuchs's activities, so much so that one report claimed he had betrayed the secret of a hormone ray that had the potential to "feminize enemy soldiers." The media also sensationalized the revelations of the more than a half-dozen FBI plants (not unlike Cvetic) who surfaced to testify in the 1949 Smith Act trial of the top CP leadership. Other trials that year gave substance to the subsequent testimony of Cvetic (and others). The Alger Hiss trials ultimately resulted in his being found guilty of perjury in January 1950 at the end of the second trial: this verdict seemed to endorse the subversion and espionage charges leveled by his prime accuser Whittaker Chambers against Hiss and by implication the CP and the Soviets. In June 1949 a jury found "government girl" Judith Coplon guilty of passing secret documents to a Soviet official; because of extralegal FBI activity the courts set this verdict aside, as well as another guilty judgment the next year; but in the press she and her Communist masters stood condemned.[6]

Domestically, happenings large and small resulted in Communists, the CP, and the Soviet Union coming under a concerted attack. These obviously did affect public opinion and served later to give substance to the charges of Cvetic and others. In August 1948 Oksanna Osenkina, a fifty-two-year-old teacher of the children of Russian diplomats, became for a moment an anti-Communist icon who "leaped to freedom." According to Soviet spokesmen, some "White Russian bandits" had "kidnapped" her, and she had been taken thirty miles from New York City to a farm from which she had been "rescued" by New York–based Soviet consular personnel who arranged for her passage back to the USSR. It seems, however, that she did not wish to return to the Soviet Union and she jumped through a window on the New York consulate's third floor, suffered fractures and "grievous" internal injuries, and over consular personnel's objections, was taken by the New York City police to a nearby hospital, and there as *Life* reported she opted for freedom, asserting "I was struggling to get out." Ms. Osenkina quickly faded from public view, the point having been made that a person would choose possible death over life in Russia. And hers was but one of many such anti-Communist stories played up by the media.[7]

In 1949, HUAC, after much-publicized hearings "regarding Communist infiltration of Radiation Laboratory and Atomic Bomb Project at the University of California," directed charges of "atomic espionage" at various Communist Party members, most notably Steve Nelson, who was singled out for his "participation." The committee, in detail, maintained that he served "the international Communist conspiracy" not just as a Party bureaucrat, which for those Congressmen, of course, was bad enough, but also as a Soviet spy, "stealing America's most valuable secrets." Cvetic in the 1950s in various venues would repeatedly give voice (and supposedly) substance to that charge.[8]

Cvetic also became for a time intimately involved with charges against Communist-dominated unions. Already in 1947 questions had been raised seriously by various union leaders and their political friends about how to stop Communist "infiltration" of organized labor, especially the Congress of Industrial Organizations (CIO), without resorting to "phony cries of Wolf! Wolf!" CP members active in the CIO were few in number but concentrated in key positions, especially among the officers and staffs of some affiliates. People may have openly guessed about the relationship of such individuals to the Party, but that membership in the main was secret and often under an assumed name (standard CP practice). That policy, as has been aptly stated, proved to be an "Achilles' heel" for hidden members—"clandestine membership" made them easy targets for persons like Cvetic.[9]

Certainly, the CIO in the 1940s one of America's two major labor organizations—did contain Communist-dominated unions. And in 1949 the CIO found it expedient to purge these affiliates from its ranks, including the United Electrical, Radio, and Machine Workers of America (colloquially known as "the UE"). It was one of the CIO's largest and most successful affiliates, "the third largest . . . following in order of size the Auto Workers and the Steel Workers" (as a UE officer proudly put it). The issue of Communists in the UE had been raised early in its history: in 1940 one labor leader going more than a bit over the top had characterized the union as "nothing more or less than a branch of the secret service of Russian dictator Joseph Stalin." The 1949 CIO convention resolution calling for expulsion mirrored that statement, declaring that the UE was "nothing more" than the "Communist Party masquerading as a labor union." Cvetic played a role in Pittsburgh during the early 1950s in the CIO's effort to establish a non-Communist union alternative to the UE.[10]

The rising tide of anti-Communism attracted many people, including, perhaps most notably, Senator Joseph McCarthy (R-Wisconsin). The senator (like Cvetic) burst onto the public scene in February 1950 during a speaking tour for the Republican Party centered on Lincoln's birthday celebrations. Capitalizing on the Communist issue, McCarthy in a speech at Wheeling, West Virginia, on February 9, spoke about "Communist agents" in the Department of State and garnered bold headlines, as did follow-up talks and press conferences in Denver, Reno, and Salt Lake City. On returning to Washington, McCarthy defended himself on the Senate floor against the massive criticism he had aroused, in a rambling, maddeningly inconsistent marathon presentation that lasted well into the night of February 20, 1950. The senator concluded just hours prior to Cvetic's initial public HUAC appearance, which began on the morning of February 21. Both Cvetic and McCarthy had joined the ongoing national heresy hunt, and both—as historian Arthur Schlesinger, Jr., has pointed out about the senator—"came late to the issue." [11]

Both men used the media, albeit Cvetic was more manipulated than manipulative. He lacked McCarthy's media savvy: as a detailed study has shown, the senator in his day "used the press in ordinary ways more effectively than anyone else." Both Cvetic and McCarthy benefited from the fact that during their heyday they operated in the shadow of the Korean War (It began in June 1950 and resulted in thousands of American casualties before the fighting ended in mid-1953. With "our boys" giving their all in a stalled war against "the Commies" in defense of freedom overseas, subversive-hunters on the home front had more leeway). The public's positive response to both men did not long outlast the war's end. Both Cvetic and McCarthy, in different ways, frittered away their careers in 1954, to a considerable extent because of acute alcoholism. Although soldiering on, they became isolated, and much to their dismay increasingly ignored as their lives wound down. [12]

And it was the phenomenon to which the senator gave his name that made it possible for Cvetic to shine briefly and which other senators such as Pat McCarran (D-Nevada) with the Internal Security Subcommittee of the Senate Judiciary Committee practiced more diligently and ruthlessly. McCarthyism, as former President Richard Nixon could attest on the basis of his experience as a member of HUAC in the late 1940s, existed before the senator hit the headlines in 1950. And as a pejorative McCarthyism exists to this day—having in Orwellian fashion escaped its red-baiting genesis. McCarthyism has become a perhaps overworked synonym for any kind of "intolerance, reckless accusations, feckless scapegoating, character assassination" (to use journalist/editor James Wechsler's definition).[13]

In a hard-fought primary during the latter half of 1946 McCarthy won the slot as GOP candidate for the U.S. Senate and scored an easy electoral triumph in November, taking his seat in the first days of January 1947. It was then that Cvetic in Pittsburgh made the contact that would propel him out of obscurity. At "Paddy's Horse Room," Cvetic made the acquaintance of James Moore—a well-connected, gregarious, genial, conservative local newsman. He had graduated from Franklin and Marshall in the early 1930s, been active in the Pittsburgh chapter of the American Newspaper Guild, and served with the Flying Tigers during World War II. Returning to Pittsburgh at war's end, he found employment with the Hearst chain's *Sun-Telegraph* and covered the City Hall beat. At one of their first meetings, Cvetic, using the pseudonym Bob Stanton, spun what the experienced newsman spotted as a "phony tale." The somewhat inebriated Cvetic, "found out," invited Moore to the William Penn, and there over drinks explained his Communist ties and FBI connection. Thereafter the two stayed in touch.[14]

During the summer of 1949, Cvetic—concerned about the quality of his relationship with the FBI and anxious to find a way to convert it into cash—approached Moore about capitalizing on his ties to the Bureau and the undercover work he had done for it. Cvetic asked Moore to peddle the story of a man who worked undercover for the FBI—a hot subject at the time because of the surfacing of FBI plants such as Philbrick and Calomiris during the Smith Act prosecution of the top CP leadership. Moore claims that then and for some time afterward he had "no inkling" of Cvetic's increasingly complex relationship with the Bureau or of its attitude toward this informant. Moore wanted his newspaper to set up an "exclusive" with Cvetic, but found that his bosses were not interested. The newspaper's management, according to Moore, "didn't want to own Cvetic," but the newsman found some people who did. He put Cvetic in touch with Blair F. Gunther and Harry Alan Sherman, possibly the most vigorous, indiscreet, and vocal of Pittsburgh's self-elected anti-Communist crusaders.[15]

The vehemently patriotic, almost obsessively anti-

Communist Gunther at that moment was a tough, popular Allegheny County judge. Appointed to the County Court in 1942 and elected to a ten-year term in 1943, Gunther had initially been dubbed "the travelin' judge," because for a while he had fulfilled his promise to "bring the law to the people" and had held court in various county communities and not just in Pittsburgh. Gunther by all accounts was a witty zestful man, who over the years had energetically practiced ethnic and fraternal politics. A Moose and an Elk, he was also an active member of Rotary and other civic groups. He was born in 1903 in west central Pennsylvania to an immigrant family of limited means. He and his sister did not have an easy childhood. Blair Gunther had come to Pittsburgh in early 1924, supposedly as a stopover on his way to Oregon to become an apple farmer. Press release after press release during his electoral campaigns had it that Gunther had lost his "bankroll" (or "last five dollars") in a poker game, and that "an old school chum talked me into going to . . . law school." He received his LL.B. in 1927 from Duquesne University and was admitted to the bar in 1928.[16]

By then he had already gone to work in the law offices of the man whose daughter he would marry. After Gunther's death in 1966 the *New York Times* acknowledged him to have been "for many years one of the most powerful men in Pennsylvania's Republican Party." However, from 1935 through 1938 Gunther served Pennsylvania's Democratic administration as a deputy attorney general in that state's Department of Justice. In 1938 he unsuccessfully sought the Democratic nomination for the House of Representatives. An ambitious man Gunther, after returning to private practice, tried again for elective office in 1942—this time as a Republican, but with no greater luck. He unsuccessfully sought the GOP nomination for Coroner of Allegheny County. Not everybody viewed Gunther's activities positively: a contemporary FBI report observed that he "has been described as a political opportunist willing to use any means to reach his end."[17]

Gunther's social origins had much in common with Cvetic's. Both of Gunther's parents had been born in Eastern Europe—in Poland, although the father's family was of German extraction. The father and mother had come separately to the United

States, met, and married. The father after coming to this country had worked as a coal miner, but with great effort had become a small businessman. Like Cvetic's father he owned and operated a hotel for a time in a medium-sized community, and subsequently went on to operate other concerns that catered to the immigrant community.[18]

The judge always emphasized his Polish roots, spoke the language fluently, and exploited his proficiency in it during his campaigns for office. A friendly newspaper profile described him as "something of a professional Pole." He well represented the anti-Communism of the many Polish-Americans outraged by Soviet actions against their homeland. In 1948 he served as state president of the Polish American Congress. In the early 1940s Gunther headed the Polish National Alliance of North America—at that time the largest Polish-American fraternal organization, with more than 300,000 members. That tie led to his involvement with the American Slav Congress, an involvement he later came to rue and which may well have heightened his anti-Communism.[19]

The genesis of the American Slav Congress remains in contention. A summary of a 1949 HUAC report details the attitude of the organization's detractors: "organized in 1942 in response to an appeal from . . . Moscow. During the war it was patriotic and pro-Soviet; since the war . . . mostly pro-Soviet, and has followed the . . . Party line with a monotonous lack of deviation." In 1954 Cvetic in this vein succinctly dismissed before a Senate Committee the American Slav Congress as "a Communist-controlled Communist-front working on Slavic groups." On the other hand over a decade earlier, at the height of World War II, the *Pittsburgh Press* said that the Congress had been created "with Government blessing" to serve as an anti-Fascist umbrella organization for the large national groups such as the Polish National Alliance and the hundreds of smaller ethnic groups: "its main purpose" was to "promote the war effort" among Eastern European workers in the United States; these workers were estimated by the government to make up 53 percent of those working in war plants, and the government felt it needed an organization to reach them. That positive wartime attitude remained the story put forth after 1945 by the adherents and defenders of the American Slav Congress, but to no avail. The Congress soon appeared on the

Attorney General's list—a popular designation for the organizations designated as subversive by the Justice Department in compliance with the 1947 Executive Order establishing a federal "loyalty program" (various states and localities incorporated the list into their loyalty programs, and private vetting agencies utilized it as well).[20]

Gunther's Polish connections as well as his ambitions led to his involvement with the founding of the American Slav Congress. He attended the April 1942 organizing meeting in Detroit (which one participant recalled ended with "nearly 10,000 gathered for a victory rally" to hear speeches by representatives from the U.S. Treasury, the War Production Board, the Department of Labor, other government agencies, and "greetings came from President Roosevelt"). Gunther was elected chairman of the new organization's board of directors, probably because of his Polish connection. In October 1943 he became a board member of a newly created Pittsburgh Council of American-Soviet Friendship. Some months later an FBI agent reported to his superiors that in his opinion Gunther's election as judge in 1943 "was . . . through the efforts of the Communist Party in this district."[21]

Gunther soon had a falling out with the Communists. Had he, as they later angrily claimed, used them and their organizations for "his personal gain"; or had his innate anti-Communism come to the fore; or did he simply exemplify the English journalist Walter Bagehot's concept of the ideal politician as a man who never entertains "ideas of unseasonable originality." Less than seven months after Gunther's election Communists charged him with being a Fascist, and worked to force him out of the American Slav Congress. They succeeded; he left, and soon was declaring everywhere "the Commies are taking over" and working against them. And he seemed to have had some success, since in April 1946 the *Daily Worker,* commenting on his efforts to oppose the American Slav Congress, called him "a stooge for former Nazi puppets."[22]

Ironically, notwithstanding such name-calling and the judge's anti-Communist efforts, his relatively brief ties to the American Slav Congress led him to be red-baited in 1950. He had been appointed to the State Superior Court in April 1950—not long after his much-publicized involvement with the surfacing of Cvetic (Gunther had reaped banner headlines for that assistance and his anti-Communism). The election for the judgeship took place in November. During the electoral campaign that summer his Democratic opponent charged him "with being the former head of a Communist-front organization" and played up Gunther's ties to the American Slav Congress. Taking a leaf out of Cvetic's book, the judge said he'd done it for the FBI, and had "letters in his possession . . . proving his contention." This was not so. Advised of Gunther's response Hoover notified the U.S. Attorney General that if requested he would inform anyone who inquired that Gunther had never "acted in any capacity for the Bureau." What action if any the administration or the Attorney General then took remains unclear. Gunther weathered the storm and in November 1950 not only won his race but led the entire GOP state ticket in votes.[23]

Like so many politicians Gunther veered further right as he grew older. By 1960 his brand of politics elicited a less favorable response, and he was defeated for reelection. The next year he was appointed prothonotary of the Superior Court in order that he might achieve the necessary tenure to become eligible for a state pension. In 1963 he was elected to the Allegheny County Commission, the minority Republican who sat with two Democrats. His glory days were behind him, and he made different headlines: one newspaper story during his days as a county commissioner was headed "Gunther Scores As He Snores." Increasingly conservative politically, he supported a proposed constitutional amendment repealing the federal income tax. In 1964 he worked to achieve the nomination of Barry Goldwater as the Republican presidential candidate (he was a delegate to the national convention), despite the fact that his own state's governor was also seeking the GOP nomination.[24]

A close ally of Gunther in many of his post–World War II anti-Communist endeavors was Harry Alan Sherman—an energetic, clever, and handsome Pittsburgh lawyer. Sherman, like the judge, campaigned strenuously and aggressively against what they considered "the Communist threat" (an obituary likened Sherman to a "tiger"). But even Sherman's allies found him a bit much. Monsignor Rice in looking back has characterized Sherman as "a rabid conservative, . . . really a bastard." Even during Sherman's most active anti-

Communist phase Bureau personnel expressed concern about his actions: in 1953 an annoyed Pittsburgh FBI agent reported to his superiors in Washington that "past experience with Sherman has shown that he has utter disregard for truth." His forays into politics over the years had proved fruitless. Even in 1955, just past the peak of his much-vaunted anti-Communism Sherman fared very poorly in a stab for the Republican nomination for Pittsburgh District Attorney.[25]

Born in Pittsburgh in 1906, the son of a respectable striving lower-middle-class Jewish family (he had two sisters, as well as a brother who participated in some of his anti-Communist activity), Sherman graduated from the University of Pittsburgh in 1929, and from its law school three years later. Although admitted to the bar in 1933 Sherman continued on in the newspaper business until 1935; he had begun as a teenager in 1925. For almost all his legal career Sherman was a sole practitioner. On reaching his early sixties Sherman spent more and more time in Coral Gables, Florida, but he remained in harness in Pittsburgh, continuing to practice there until his death from cancer in 1987. A fellow member of the bar recalled that "there was always a phone number where you could reach Harry in Pittsburgh."[26]

Sherman was remembered as "a hell of a good litigator" and a "plaintiff's lawyer"; his practice generally involved low-level litigation. After his death the practice was described as "delving into . . . labor law, . . . domestic relations, and criminal work." He would defend a man charged with "withholding money collected while working for the Internal Revenue Service," speak for a client before the state Pardon Board, represent residents "battling" the building in their neighborhood of integrated housing. Sherman did not hesitate to sail too close to the wind. In the mid-1940s, for example, Pittsburgh postal authorities contemplated action against Sherman because of what an FBI agent called "certain illegal and irregular practices" in violation of "existing postal regulations" in conjunction with soliciting advertising for the *Keystone Republican,* a political sheet, during a 1946 primary campaign. Sherman sidestepped dire consequences by signing a "statement promising to cease the practice immediately."[27]

He seems to have been fearless, working as a lawyer on behalf of individuals or groups in Pittsburgh who challenged labor racketeers. At one point in the early 1940s he was deeply involved in legal actions against such less than savory personalities as the Hod Carriers' Nick Stirone—whom he charged with "extortion"—and the Teamsters' Anthony F. Bianco (a.k.a. "Buck White"), whose response in court to evidence that he had been "on the take" was that he had been "framed." In both cases Sherman was attempting to halt the return to office of men known for using a union position for what a Pittsburgh judge described as "a racket for their own benefit." Along with that fearlessness went a never ending contentiousness, which led judges to caution him about his volatile conduct and to order the modification of his pleadings because of their intemperate "scurrilous" language. Any number of times the possibility of fights with opposing counsel arose; Sherman never backed off; when threatened with "a punch in the nose" he invited his adversary to go "right ahead . . . you'll get a lot of punches back."[28]

Already during World War II Sherman's outspoken anti-Communism had attracted attention. Around 1940 he had begun to serve as a part-time business and legal adviser to various union locals, the functions that had brought him into court combating labor racketeering. He worked mostly with smaller locals. Among them was a Pittsburgh UE local, part of that union's District 6 (made up of UE members in western Pennsylvania, and including some of the union's largest, most important locals). After the June 1941 German attack on Russia, the UE, like other formerly militant Communist-dominated CIO unions, had promised "an all-out effort to increase production" and adopted a "no-strike" policy.[29]

One of the locals Sherman represented in mid-1943 challenged that policy when, because of discontent over hours, wages, and conditions, it "participated in a work stoppage" (to use the wording of District 6's secretary-treasurer in a letter he sent to the FBI in order to call the Bureau's attention to Sherman and to request an investigation). In the end District 6 booted Sherman out of the UE and off its council, as well as suspending the local. But Sherman remained an irritant: the District 6 head said that he was giving the union "many headaches," and in January 1945 a special meeting of the UE general executive board was held in New York City, primarily, said an FBI report, to discuss Sherman's activities. During 1944–45 members of three locals under Sherman's tutelage won certification elections establishing them outside the UE as "independent bargaining groups." In early November 1944 Sherman sued fifteen UE and District 6 officers asking for redress because they were part of "a Communist conspiracy" plotting "against the constitutional government of the United States." One issue of the newspaper he oversaw for these locals had a front-page headline in bold black large-size type "RATS AT WORK" and attacked "UE (Dis)Organizers," described Communists as "the most brazen liars in the world," and blistered "District Six Rats." Notwithstanding the abeyance of red-baiting during America's World War II love feast with the Soviets, Sherman's lawsuit got wide play (even making its way in detail into the *New York Times,* not then much given to coverage of local legal actions in western Pennsylvania).[30]

Sherman won a series of battles in addition to the representation elections. Another of the locals he advised, despite warnings from the District 6 leadership, went out on strike. Indeed Sherman remained such an irritant to the UE that, according to the reports of FBI confidential informants, concerned Communist "officials" intervened. Ultimately Sherman lost the war: at the end of January 1945 the UE obtained an injunction restraining him (a temporary order later made permanent), and in March 1945 an Allegheny County court dismissed his lawsuit because the judge found "at least one-half" of Sherman's complaint "consisted of impertinent, irrelevant, and scandalous material."[31]

There can be no doubt, then or later, about the intensity of Sherman's anti-Communism. In the long run, however, that intensity led him to making overwrought and uncorroboratable exaggerations: always given to hyperbole, as the years wore on, his charges became more and more outrageous. In 1953, for example, he told a Senate committee investigating the supposed subversive influence of the UE that the Communists "took credit" for the death of a "man who was going to do some talking to the Government" about the UE. The man had been blown to pieces ("just parts of his body were adhering to the walls, just specks"). And how had this been accomplished? Sherman testified that the Communists said "they did it" by putting "in his lunch box a bomb that could be detonated by the magnetic wavelengths of the generating plant where they knew he would pass on the way to his job." Sherman added, "They also . . . put the kiss of death on me." [32]

A volatile mixture of deep emotional concern and ruthless self-aggrandizing ambition seems to have sparked such testimony. His critics focused only on the self-aggrandizing ambition, and cited among other things his assault on Pittsburgh's Yiddish Kultur Farband (Jewish Cultural Association) in the first half of the 1950s. Sherman's detractors decried his charges that the Communists "abused . . . the Jewish faith" and attempted to use it as "a shield." Active in local Jewish community affairs, Sherman asserted that his vociferous anti-Communist activity stemmed not only from patriotic grounds but also from his belief that Communists in Pittsburgh and elsewhere paid only lip service to religious tolerance; for him they, like their Soviet masters, were "very anti-Semitic." [33]

Sherman attacked the Yiddish Kultur Farband (YKF) as a "Communist front" that in order to "disguise its sinister activities . . . veiled itself in the body and sacred traditions of the Jewish religion." Cvetic on surfacing had also described the YKF as a training ground for Communists. By 1953 its parent organization, the Jewish Culture Society, had been added to the Attorney General's list. In April 1953 during the Passover holidays Sherman petitioned the courts to revoke the YKF charter. In July of that year Sherman led a raid on the YKF's headquarters building, described by a Pittsburgh newspaper "as a staid and impressive gray-stoned manse . . . in the heart of . . . an exclusive residential district." Sherman and six others (among them a "borrowed" police photographer to record any evidence indicating Communist activity, and the lawyer's brother, who happened to be running for the city council) descended on the building in search of subversive material to support the suit to revoke the YKF's charter. What they found (e.g., Red Army songbooks, copies of Communist newspapers and pamphlets, books dealing with Russian life, and application blanks for the International Workers Order, an organization charged with being Communist dominated), said Sherman, "unmasked the center as a school for young Communists."[34]

During his campaign to have the YKF's charter revoked, Sherman was appointed a special assistant to the state's attorney general. In January 1955 a local judge did revoke that charter, the authorities "padlocked" the building and took possession of the YKF's assets, and a trustee was appointed to liquidate them. As critics of Sherman pointed out, at a lucrative fee he became counsel to the trustee, a position he did not hold for very long. By mid-June 1955 a newly elected state attorney general had dismissed him, and declared that both Sherman and YKF counsel Hyman Schlesinger were more concerned with vilifying each other, speechmaking, and newspaper headlines than with the "accomplishment of a speedy determination of the justice in the case."[35]

Sherman and Gunther, however one views their attributes or shortcomings, were typical of the anti-Communists in Pittsburgh in the years immediately preceding the surfacing of Cvetic. Moore's approaching them on Cvetic's behalf made good sense for everyone concerned. Americans Battling Communism, Inc. (ABC), the Pittsburgh organization that was Cvetic's ostensible sponsor and that paid his travel expenses from western Pennsylvania to Washington, D.C., for his initial HUAC appearance, had been a creation of both Sherman and Gunther. In the immediate aftermath of World War II, the Soviet oppression of Eastern Europe, and the increasing domestic fear of Communism, the judge had been involved with the creation of various organizations such as the "Committee to Stop World Communism" and the "United American Organization Against Communism." Despite the involvement of some prominent people, a left-wing Detroit Polish newspaper correctly later described these organizations as "stillborn."[36]

Americans Battling Communism, Inc., aptly characterized as a "pressure group," actually functioned for a while. Those whom it attacked argued that ABC was an "instrument of political repression" and "a vigilante group." These phrases are something of an exaggeration, but even if Gunther, Sherman, and their associates would have objected to such terms, they certainly saw nothing wrong in hounding those they considered Communists. But for much of its existence Americans Battling Communism was not much more than a façade that Sherman used to enhance his own prestige: thus, a press release would be sent out by Sherman, identifying him as the "chairman of Americans Battling Communism: who would address the members of (you name it) on 'Communists in Our Midst' (or a similar topic)." ABC has also been described as a "mysterious organization, not least in its original inspiration." But such does not seem to be the case. It had been conceived in early October 1947 as the result of anxiety by some practitioners of fraternal ethnic politics in western Pennsylvania over what they called an "outlandish" convention of the Croatian Fraternal Union that had resulted in what were called "Red elements" gaining control of that organization.[37]

Gunther, along with some other concerned individuals, had called together some fifty like-minded people ("civic leaders" the press called them) to discuss ways of combating such infiltration. They met one night in his courtroom, among them were some county court judges, the Recorder of Deeds, a few medium-rank police officers, a former U.S. Attorney, the head of the local Reserve Officers Association, Sherman, and John Ladesic—who had led the anti-Communist fight in the recent Croatian Fraternal Union. They adopted what was called "the Pittsburgh plan against Communism," which by "educating" the public to its thrust would "expose the Reds." Gunther in his statement emphasized the "educational" aspects, calling it an "ABC movement," an acronym that gave birth to Americans Battling Communism. Sherman quickly filed for a charter as a "non-profit organization to combat Communism." That charter was granted at the end of November 1947.[38]

During the weeks that passed between requesting and getting a charter the fledgling organization embarrassed itself. One of its members, a candidate for the bench in the upcoming election, had prevailed upon ABC "to screen the contending candidates" for subversive tendencies. Sherman, advised by various local anti-Communists that HUAC had reams of information readily available, wrote the congressional committee. HUAC did not have much on file. The probe made clear only that "one of the candidates" for judge was "foreign born," and that another "allegedly was once associated with a group advocating friendship" between the USSR and the United States and had been "a member of a citizens group that communicated with Russian women during the war." Sherman admitted that "we were completely taken in" and that the ABC member who had called for the screening had obviously done so, not to combat Communism but simply to discredit an electoral rival. Americans Battling Communism, in the words of two spokesmen, had been "euchred" and made to look silly. Some took a stronger response. The *Pittsburgh Press,* which specifically took Sherman to task for his cupidity, editorialized that the attorney's effort was "the most malicious brand of innuendo" as well as "the cheesiest piece of work." [39]

The ABC charter called for it to "formulate and execute . . . [an] aggressive program for enlightening American people as to the purpose, the methods, and the agencies of the Communist organization to the end that an enlightened and alerted public . . . shall take such steps, including . . . security legislation as may be necessary to eliminate the threat posed by Communism to the American way of life." The organization was intended, at least initially, to be educational. It proved to be a bit more because of some adherents like Sherman. In October 1950 during Judge Gunther's state-wide campaign for judicial office, Americans Battling Communism organized what proved to be a short-lived Philadelphia chapter. Even Hoover noted the "possibility that Judge Gunther may use the chapter for political purposes." Almost a year earlier newsman Moore had approached Gunther and Sherman successfully about Cvetic's potentialities. Things did not ultimately work out as any of them planned. But Americans Battling Communism got a boost, albeit not one totally in tune with its stated educational mission, when Cvetic surfaced in February 1950. [40]

Americans Battling Communism deserves attention despite its obvious limitations, despite being as much a front organization as the Communist groups it claimed to battle and to expose. J. Edgar Hoover seems to have understood well that ABC was a way for a few politically ambitious persons to get on the anti-Communist bandwagon, whatever the sincerity of their anti-Red beliefs. But whatever ABC's shortcomings it gave Cvetic and his handlers the chance to surface him with a respectable patina. ABC provided Cvetic with seemingly responsible sponsors, necessary (if limited) financial aid, and useful entrée to the public scene. Neither ABC as a group nor Sherman and Gunther as individuals gained much from their association with Cvetic, but Cvetic got the launch he wanted, which gave him national exposure (and the possibility of hoped-for financial rewards). One could even say that ABC helped to create a monster and like Dr. Frankenstein it found this monster ungrateful and unmanageable.

three

The Myths

The U.S. census recorded Pennsylvania's population as 10,498,012 in 1950, the year that Cvetic surfaced. According to FBI head J. Edgar Hoover, in the summer of 1950 less than one-tenth of one percent of the state's population formally belonged to the Party: he said that Pennsylvania's CP could claim only 2,875 members (and the Director seems to have included in that total the numerous FBI plants such as Cvetic). Presumably there was an exactitude to Hoover's comments, since the FBI scrutinized all CP functions and publications and monitored Party activities using electronic surveillance, surreptitious entry, and infiltration. Hoover in referring to the Communist menace also conjured up a larger number, living in the shadows. He (and others) also argued that "behind the Party . . ." stood a half-million fellow travelers and sympathizers ready to do the Communist bidding.[1]

Cvetic in his often marathon HUAC appearances in 1950 (he testified for three full days in February, and over a half-dozen times thereafter during the rest of the year) named more than three hundred people as active in Communist efforts in western Pennsylvania. Obviously, that many names represented a significant portion of those in the area affiliated with the Party, its fronts of one kind or another, and causes it embraced. HUAC loved names, it thrived on them. The FBI worked closely with HUAC (and other congressional antisubversive committees such as those chaired by Senators McCarran and McCarthy) suggesting names. FBI cooperation included systematic briefings of committee staff as well as making available supposedly restricted confidential information from the FBI's voluminous files. It was not just happenstance that "Communist Infiltration of the Motion Picture Industry" was not only the title the Los Angeles Bureau gave to its many 1940s and 1950s reports to Hoover but also the designation HUAC used for its 1951–52 hearings dealing with filmmakers. The FBI also provided a flow of friendly witnesses: according to historian Kenneth O'Reilly these witnesses were the "lifeblood" of HUAC. Not all its "friendly" witnesses were former FBI plants. Some like Louis Budenz (CP functionary and former managing editor of the *Daily Worker,* the Communist newspaper) had defected—but a significant number during HUAC's heyday were, like Cvetic, individuals the FBI had utilized over the years to infiltrate the CP.[2]

The Bureau certainly had nothing to do with Cvetic's surfacing. Moreover, it does not seem to have hindered him or HUAC before or after he testified in 1950. The Bureau could be vindictive—its subsequent treatment of Cvetic, deserved or not, demonstrates that willingness and capacity. Nothing in the released FBI files dealing with this moment in time indicate any Bureau activity against Cvetic. However, it is important to note that not released were eighty pages following an "addendum" that reported that Louis Russell, a senior HUAC investigator, had "telephonically" advised the Bureau on the evening of Friday, February 17, that Cvetic had been subpoenaed, would appear before the committee the next morning in executive session, and "will be called before a public hearing," Tuesday, February 21. Other sources also informed the Bureau of Cvetic's surfacing.[3]

It does appear, that then and for at least a few months thereafter the Pittsburgh Bureau was relieved to be rid of Cvetic. FBI headquarters may have likewise had a sense of relief, but it was also irritated that the media was referring to Cvetic as an agent rather than as a confidential informant. Hoover's notations on press clippings dealing with Cvetic's HUAC testimony are concerned in detail with this issue. He also repeatedly inquired in marginal annotations, "Did Cvetic ever report this incident?" and "Was any such information given us by Cvetic?"[4]

The FBI had some inkling that Cvetic would ultimately embarrass the Bureau. It knew about his drinking, although just then he had it more or less under control. But initially the FBI treated him discreetly. The Bureau forwarded the mail his celebrity status had engendered: after being read and copied, these letters were according to Hoover's instructions "re-mailed to Cvetic in a plain envelope without any clarifying communication from the Bureau." But well before the end of 1950 Cvetic's antics had so embarrassed and angered the Pittsburgh Bureau that it recommended that the FBI divorce itself from him totally. Among other incidents that occasioned this recommendation was a drunk Cvetic's run-in with the Pittsburgh police, who telephoned the Pittsburgh FBI; given the circumstances it felt compelled to respond that "this office had no comment to make." Hoover said he agreed with the regional office's recommendations. Further indiscretions on Cvetic's part reinforced that decision, which meant that even though the FBI kept close tabs on Cvetic until his death in 1962, ultimately any inquiry about Cvetic would be answered "Please be advised . . . his current address is unknown."[5]

Just how Cvetic came to HUAC's attention remains less than clear. The process involved others besides Moore, Sherman, and Gunther–although they benefited the most from Cvetic's surfacing. Somehow, while dealing with Moore and Sherman (and perhaps through them), Cvetic aroused the interest of *Pittsburgh Press* newsman Robert Taylor, who in 1947 had penned a multipart exposé of "the Communist presence" in the area's ethnic organizations. Either he or Gunther or both knew Courtney Owens, who had been with HUAC for five years as an investigator and process server. The sequence, according to Cvetic a year later, went as follows: Cvetic told Taylor that he "was available to testify"; Taylor called Owens; and Owens told Cvetic "when to come down." Meanwhile, before speaking with Taylor, Cvetic had spoken with Sherman, apparently at the instigation of Moore, and Sherman contacted Gunther. All this seems to have taken place in January as the FBI "discontinued" Cvetic.[6]

Sherman, because of his stake in Americans Battling Communism, had a special interest in Cvetic apart from any other con-

siderations. The lawyer later said that he trained Cvetic "like a soldier" so he would know what to say and what not to say. Sherman
had a "low regard" for Cvetic's intelligence and moral character and
felt that the former FBI informant had "delusions of grandeur." Sherman had hoped to profit financially from Cvetic as well as use him to
bolster the GOP's 1950 electoral fortunes in western Pennsylvania
generally, and Gunther's specifically. Sherman brought Cvetic to
Gunther, who at the time (early 1950), had at least some hope of becoming the GOP candidate for governor. Gunther saw in Cvetic a
way to hitch a ride on the increasingly popular anti-Communist
bandwagon, assuming correctly that Cvetic's upcoming HUAC appearances would generate a great deal of media attention, which
they did.[7]

Gunther secretly "deposed" Cvetic on February 7. Eleven
days later he released this deposition to the press (i.e., Taylor and
Moore), just *after* Cvetic, with $200 or $300 expense money provided by Americans Battling Communism, had left by train for
Washington, D.C., to meet with HUAC personnel. Neither Taylor
nor Moore overlooked the judge's role in Cvetic's surfacing. As Taylor dramatically put it, Cvetic "testified under oath at a secret hearing
in Pittsburgh February 7 . . . before Judge Blair F. Gunther . . .
founder of Americans Battling Communism." Next to Taylor's story
was a two-column photo supposedly taken on February 7 showing,
as the caption said, "Gunther swearing in Cvetic just before a secret
hearing in Pittsburgh."[8]

This story broke just as Cvetic's associates wanted it to, both
in the press and on the radio (in a special thirty-minute broadcast
prepared just before Cvetic went to Washington). The script, apparently written by Moore, began: "This special broadcast tonight is
being aired in the hope that you the listening public will become
more aware of the dangers and the workings of the Communist
Party." The broadcast introduced Cvetic as a heroic FBI counterspy,
eulogized him, and asserted that his story "rival[ed] any fictional
thriller on the radio." For most of his subsequent public life Cvetic
parroted what Moore wrote for the broadcast, true or not. The
broadcast declared that Cvetic had sacrificed his family life in pursuit of the defense of his country, and the broadcast maintained that

Matt Cvetic (right) and George Dietze after the latter surfaced, unable to stand the gaff of being named by Cvetic as a member of the Communist Party.

(Courtesy, Pittsburgh Post-Gazette Archives)

Matt Cvetic (left) and Harry Alan Sherman pose with literature discovered in a raid on what one newspaper called "an alleged Red meeting house." Cvetic is holding a "telephonic transmitting device" found on the premises.

(Courtesy, Pittsburgh Post-Gazette Archives)

Matt Cvetic, at the height of his fame, when *I Was a Communist for the FBI* premiered in Pittsburgh.

(Courtesy, Pittsburgh Post-Gazette Archives)

Matt Cvetic (left) with his "sailor son Richard" (as one newspaper put it),
during a break in his initial HUAC testimony in Washington, D.C.

(Courtesy, Pittsburgh Post-Gazette Archives)

Matt Cvetic, having returned to Pittsburgh after his successful initial
HUAC testimony in February 1951, is congratulated upon entering his
hotel home there.

(Courtesy, Carnegie Library of Pittsburgh)

Matt Cvetic (left) and his father on St. Patrick's Day, 1950.

(Courtesy, Pittsburgh Post-Gazette Archives)

Matt Cvetic (left) with his son Matt Jr., in mid-1950, outside a meeting room during a break in his attack on various Pittsburgh Communists.

(Courtesy, Pittsburgh Post-Gazette Archives)

LOS ANGELES EVENING AND SUNDAY

HERALD EXAMINER

★

Tuesday, Aug. 21, 1962

Herbert H. Krauch, Editor

D-2
George R. Hearst Jr., Publisher

Matt Cvetic, a Real Hero

Some men become heroes on the battlefields of war, others on the battlefields of peace. Matt Cvetic, who died in Los Angeles recently from a heart attack, was one of the latter.

At the request of the FBI, Cvetic became a Communist to spy on the Reds and learn their secrets. In that he did a tremendous job and the Communists never learned they had been tricked until Cvetic went on the witness stand and told his story before a congressional committee.

But in the meantime, what suffering he went through in life. He could not reveal to anyone including his closest relatives why he had become a Communist.

His Austrian immigrant mother died in sorrow in 1949 believing her son to be a traitor to the United States. His father only learned the truth three months before he died.

When Cvetic's wife learned he was a Communist she took their twin sons and left him, eventually divorcing him.

Matt Cvetic, in our opinion, was a great hero. He made the supreme sacrifice in life. May kind memories of him and what he did for his country remain in our hearts forever.

Cvetic's death did not go unnoticed. This editorial eulogized him, and in so doing reiterates the various myths that mark the Cvetic story, as, for example, the collapse of his family life because of his FBI activity.

Cvetic left FBI service after being "prevailed upon to move out in the open" by Gunther and Sherman. Cvetic, in Moore's words, reported on his Party activities and the "violent danger" to the United States that the CP represented.[9]

A thirty-minute broadcast could only say so much, although it did manage more than once to excoriate CP leader Steve Nelson, who, it said, "has been accused of passing atomic secrets . . . to the Russians" and of referring "to the U.S. Government as the enemy." The newspapers repeated some of the broadcast but emphasized Cvetic's February 7 deposition, presenting it at great length and playing up every possible anti-Communist angle. Like the radio broadcast, the initial newspaper stories had a kind of breathless revelatory quality. In the broadcast Cvetic "sacrifices" for his country, but with more space available in print than thirty broadcast minutes allowed, he told all. It was frightening, according to his testimony, what the Red Menace had accomplished and planned to do.[10]

As reported in the press, Cvetic had told Judge Gunther that Communism prescribed "violent revolution," that Steve Nelson had been sent to Pittsburgh as a Party leader because the Communists recognized the area's "strategic importance" and were "now concentrating on . . . U.S. Steel," and that Communist interest in trade unions was "to utilize them as an instrument for overthrowing the U.S. Government." Under what one newspaper tactfully referred to as "questioning by Harry Alan Sherman, attorney and member of Americans Battling Communism," Cvetic said the Party "operated as a 'fifth column' among Slavic and other nationality groups," that three of Pittsburgh's Slavic newspapers took their marching orders from Party leaders, that Communists were "concentrating on . . . organization in the Progressive Party," and that the CP had organized "smear attacks" on anti-Communist public officials such as Judge Gunther."[11]

In 1950 Cvetic appeared as a witness before HUAC on eleven separate occasions (February 21, 22, 23; March 13, 14, 24, 25; June 22; September 28; and October 13 and 21).[12] Cvetic's "record performance" (as one critic put it) had a quality of outspoken freshness at first but eventually became repetitive, less straightforward, and dogmatic. Like so many who exist in the public eye only because they have a story to tell, Cvetic soon began to embellish and exaggerate his testimony. He felt the need (as has been artfully pointed out by civil liberties attorney Frank Donner in a different context) for "the creation of new stories when the truth is used up." One such invention that failed to catch the popular imagination dealt with what the Pittsburgh dailies called "the jalopy papers," material found in an auto that had crashed, injuring its passengers and fatally injuring its driver. Police found enough lists, canceled checks, pamphlets, and the like in the car to fill a large suitcase, which they sent off to HUAC, since the material revealed "many activities of the Red youth movement in the Pittsburgh area." Cvetic was called on to examine the material before testifying on Communist infiltration of U.S. college life. But even in the overheated atmosphere of the day Cvetic's interpretation of the "draft principles" underlying the Labor Youth League, a nascent Communist youth organization, lacked impact, and "the jalopy papers" faded away.[13]

Once Cvetic surfaced, Hoover was immediately concerned about the FBI's stake in his credibility. The Director ordered the Pittsburgh Bureau to evaluate in detail, on the basis of Cvetic's reports, his February and March HUAC testimony, which had captured so many headlines. One "analysis and review" that the Pittsburgh Bureau sent Hoover took up over thirty-five single-spaced typed pages. Ultimately the Pittsburgh Bureau, referring to the February and March hearings, reported to Hoover that "Cvetic's testimony when considered on a broad basis and in its entirety, is fairly accurate but in many instances . . . contains . . . misstatements compared with reports submitted by him." In Washington, D.C., one of Hoover's close associates glossed over any problems and, after a review, concluded that Cvetic's testimony "was generally accurate in light of information available to Pittsburgh from other reliable sources."[14]

Hoover had ordered the Pittsburgh Bureau to evaluate Cvetic's testimony on the basis of the reports in order to ascertain whether he had exaggerated after the fact. Probably not much, for as one FBI official with good insight argued, many of the misstatements just resulted from "Cvetic's attempt to overemphasize his importance and dramatize his testimony." Moreover, it seems that Cvetic (understandably) had not kept copies of any of his reports. That may also account for some of the misstatements. Further, it does not seem unreasonable for him to lack total recall about the contents of so many pages of reports submitted over so long a period of time. Of course, and unfortunately, such lapses of memory as did occur did not interfere with his positive and sometimes damning responses to the questions asked during the hearings by committee members and staff. Only rarely did Cvetic admit, "I can't say yes or no to that." Perhaps Hoover should have raised questions about the validity of the reports. But in the main they just seem to have been very prosaic accounts of meetings with names, dates, and the like.[15]

The FBI had told HUAC investigator Louis Russell just before Cvetic's initial appearance that the informant "would make a good witness." And certainly Cvetic did—at first. In February and March 1950 Cvetic elaborated without much embellishment on what he had told Gunther earlier. Responding to questions about what HUAC counsel termed "the Communist presence in western Pennsylvania," Cvetic spoke at length about various organizations that the committee claimed the Communists dominated. These organizations, as might be expected, included the American Slav Congress and the Progressive Party. Cvetic also spent considerable time testifying about what HUAC called "Communist infiltration of labor unions"; he focused particularly on the UE and its important Pittsburgh local. The workplaces that Local 601 had organized and represented had become bitterly contested terrain between the UE (savaged by its opponents as "a Communist-dominated" union) and those who would replace it with another CIO-backed union.[16]

The only glitch in the well-orchestrated proceedings has interesting overtones. While over the weekend of February 18–19 committee staff dealt with Cvetic in Washington, two HUAC investigators flew to Pittsburgh to pick up the mass of material Cvetic had collected and Sherman had "organized." Depending on the account, the two suitcases stuffed with material dealing with organizations such as the American Slav Congress, the International Workers Order, and the Progressive Party weighed either eighty or ninety-three pounds. But whatever the weight the material soon mysteriously proved shy a folder detailing the support that the American

Slav Congress had proffered public officials and politicians since 1945; much of this support had taken place since the organization had been tagged unofficially and then formally as Communist-controlled. At least one newsman said the missing file contained "political dynamite" and reported that one of those documents never submitted was the mail record of the Michigan Democratic Congressman who "at taxpayer expense" distributed "free Communist propaganda" put out by a Slav Congress leader. A Republican congressman, whose comments obviously were pointed at Democratic control of both Congress and HUAC, said the strange thing about the whole affair was that the only missing document from all those pounds of records was the one naming the congressman involved with the American Slav Congress. The congressman in question was later identified as George O. Sadowski (D-Michigan), a Detroiter with loose ties to the American Slav Congress. HUAC and the media however quickly dropped the matter of the missing file.[17]

During these hearings Cvetic named dozens of men and women as Party members or individuals with strong Communist leanings. The Party's policy of secret membership had played into its enemy's hands. Cvetic's outing of numerous persons not suspected as being subject to Party discipline hampered some very good and respectable causes that these people happened to support. In addition to giving HUAC an unusually long list of names, Cvetic also detailed the allegedly "subversive activities" of various Communist leaders in western Pennsylvania. He singled out Steve Nelson, the veteran functionary who took charge of the Party's activities in western Pennsylvania in 1948. Cvetic became Nelson's bête noire, appearing as a witness for the federal government in a Smith Act prosecution and for Pennsylvania in state sedition trials that sent the CP leader to prison. Nelson later angrily dubbed Cvetic "Pittsburgh's Number 1 informer." Then and later Nelson dismissed Cvetic's HUAC testimony as "just plain wild . . . nothing . . . other than giving names."[18]

Others besides Cvetic had been informers, had mentioned many of the same names, had discussed Communist participation in various organizations, and had dwelt on the intricate and involved relationship between the UE and the Communists. Some of these witnesses, in their testimony before HUAC, had done so more knowledgeably and intelligently, but none to that point had done so in such seeming detail and with, it seemed, an FBI imprimatur. As Walter Goodman (an even-handed historian of HUAC's activities) later pointed out, the committee "relied heavily" on Cvetic's lengthy testimony. The day Cvetic began testifying in executive session, HUAC "sources" told the media that when "his full story is told publicly it will literally smash the Communist Party in western Pennsylvania." Some months later, the committee reporting on its 1950 activities highlighted this "exposé" of the CP and asserted that Cvetic's testimony was "vitally important" in exposing the Party's "operations." [19]

Cvetic did not deserve the accolades then lavished upon him, including references as "a man of skill and intelligence" who had "demonstrated . . . courage and . . . patriotism." Still, Cvetic should not be dismissed as "a degenerate . . . barfly" and a "mercenary liar and sneak." Cvetic's defenders and detractors have both missed the point. He was very much a man of his time. The Pittsburgh newspapers that boldly headlined that Cvetic was to testify before HUAC also prominently featured stories about the sentencing by a Hungarian court of American businessman Robert Vogeler who had been pressured to plead guilty to "sabotage and spying," and about the United States breaking off diplomatic relations with Bulgaria because that country refused "to withdraw spy conspiracy charges" against a U.S. diplomat. The adulation Cvetic enjoyed after his HUAC testimony in February and March 1950 was very much part of the media spin that (whether accurately or not) countered the propaganda emanating from behind the Iron Curtain. Cvetic's story, as a prominent civil-liberties attorney later bemoaned, "dominated the front pages of the Pittsburgh papers and filled the . . . air waves for weeks." [20]

The cachet given Cvetic allowed him much greater latitude than he deserved or was capable of handling. It allowed him to damage the lives and careers of a disparate group of people, many of whom although close to or in the Party were far from being hardcore operatives like Nelson. However, before we deal with the pain Cvetic inflicted, we should ask, as Joseph Starobin (then foreign editor of the *Daily Worker* and a veteran Party member) did later, whether Communists might "not have been better off *politically,* in terms of their *image,* to assert their affiliations, to proclaim them instead of asserting their right to keep them private."[21]

CP policy at the time played into the hands of those who would use a Cvetic to "expose" Party members. Maybe Communist ties should not have made a difference, but they did—especially when originally those ties had not been known. Thus, the popular head of a steelworkers union local—in all probability properly identified as a Communist by Cvetic—was ousted by its members. And why? Because as one of them declared, "Frank . . . has never indicated he was a Communist. . . . I have dropped him like a hot potato." Surprisingly, even a quarter century later Steve Nelson seemed reluctant to discuss the affiliation of people whose politics had long since become public knowledge.[22]

The temper of the media in 1950 favored Cvetic: as the *Pittsburgh Press* put it, there "has been no room for doubt at any time about the veracity of Matt Cvetic." So he named names with virtual impunity, the newspapers presented them along with addresses (and, where known, places of employment), and the repercussions followed. So much so that the *Pittsburgh Press* felt compelled to run prominently in oversized type a story titled "Unfortunately There Are Two Andrew Ondas." The "non-Communist Andy" told the newspaper that he and his family had not " had a day of peace" since an Onda was named by Cvetic and listed by the press. The paper felt it needed to make clear "he isn't" and then went on to give the address of the "Communist Onda."[23]

Understandably, as another Pittsburgh newspaper reported, people became "jittery" over the possibility of being tagged with "Cvetic's Red label." To cite just a few examples of what could happen: Max Mandel, a violinist with the Pittsburgh Symphony, was dropped from the musicians' union, which effectively terminated his relationship with the orchestra (his case was later noted as "the first time a musician had been fired . . . for allegedly being a Communist"); Dorothy Albert, an eighteen-year veteran high school English teacher, denied being a Communist but admitted to Cvetic's charge of belonging to a front organization and was fired; "Toni" Nuss—

twenty-eight years old, with two children, on relief, a resident of a city housing project—was named by Cvetic, dubbed a "Red Queen" by the press, and ultimately had her relief payments halved by a judge who "self-righteously" (her brother's phrase) felt her children deserved support even if she did not; Martin Sumrak, a parks laborer alleged by Cvetic to be a Communist, was suspended by the Allegheny County Maintenance Employees Union and the county commissioner "until such time as he clears himself." The Communists were a legal political party but Communism and its adherents were becoming anathema, especially in a heavily Catholic and ethnic community, many of whose citizens were concerned about the brutal repression of their Church in "the old country."[24]

Ironically, an excellent manifestation of the intense pressure generated by the media was the flushing out of another FBI plant. In the past Cvetic had intimated to the Pittsburgh Bureau that he "suspected several CP members in the area as maintaining their Party membership for the purpose of informing" for the FBI. One such individual, whom Cvetic unknowingly put on the spot, was George Dietze, a German immigrant who had come to the United States in 1923 at age twenty-four. A jewelry engraver by trade he spoke "halting English." He felt the Communists had "paved the way for Hitler and his gang." In 1940 during the days of the Hitler-Stalin Pact, the FBI recruited him. He had drawn the attention of the Bureau because he contacted it to report suspicions about political goings-on at a neighborhood bookshop. Dietze, like Cvetic, worked his way into the good graces of the Communists, and in 1944 accepted an invitation to join the Party. Thereafter, his workplace (on which the FBI paid $200 a month rent) served as a Communist meeting room. The Bureau wired the space, which seated about thirty people comfortably and, according to one newspaper report, "recorded more than 550 secret sessions" over six years.[25]

Despite all his Communist activity, Dietze had not been generally known as a Party member. Once named by Cvetic, with all the attendant publicity, Dietze and his wife found their lives, in her word, "torture." They found that "once friendly neighbors turned frosty"; he lost long-standing clients; she was "afraid to go out of the house" because people would shout "Hooray for Stalin." Within two weeks after Cvetic named him Dietze had severed his relationship with the FBI, made public his connection with the Bureau, and had spoken out against what he called (perhaps with a touch of help) "the Red Fascists." [26]

Cvetic, because of the hue and cry his much-publicized anti-Communist testimony had aroused, quickly became involved with the hard-fought union representation elections that the UE's opponents hoped would result in its being replaced as the bargaining agent. The anti-UE forces, as one historian later judged, "pulled out all the stops." Looking back on such campaigns years later, Monsignor Rice expressed "regret" at what he and some other anti-Communists had done: "I was more of an unblinking . . . patriot than I should have been." He certainly was an uncompromising one then, advising his followers not to "be afraid of being called a Red-baiter." [27]

The battle against Communist influence in Pittsburgh's labor movement focused on the UE, and what Monsignor Rice has called "the eye of the storm" centered on the ultimately successful campaign to break the Communist hold on the massive Local 601 of UE District 6. The challenge came from the newly established International Union of Electrical, Radio, and Machine Workers (familiarly known as the IUE). Created by the CIO in the wake of its purge of Communist unions such as the UE, the IUE worked hard in Pittsburgh and elsewhere to capture that established union's membership. In Pittsburgh one instrument of the anti-UE campaign was Cvetic, who was sent into the fray in order to use his newfound anti-Communist celebrity to win support for the IUE. It organized a "hero's welcome" for him after his first return from Washington. The overflow crowd of about 1,200 heard Cvetic condemn the UE and declare that the "UE's interest in you was dishonest . . . the only interest they had . . . was to help overthrow the government." Monsignor Rice recalls Cvetic urging workers not to vote for "a Communist UE." Ultimately, by what has been called "a razor thin margin," the UE won this particular crucial representation election, although it would lose many others. [28]

Also involved in that anti-UE campaign was Michael Musmanno, an outspoken anti-Communist. Much to Sherman's anger and dismay Cvetic and Musmanno hit it off. Within a year the Republican Sherman felt that the Democrat Musmanno had successfully wooed Cvetic away from the GOP. In March 1951 Sherman expressed bitter disappointment: he believed Cvetic could be used for "drumming up votes with anti-Communist propaganda," and Sherman had "wanted to have Cvetic's influence in this connection placed at the disposal of Republicans, not the Democrats." The ultimate break, however, came over money, and in mid-1953 Sherman and Cvetic had an acrimonious falling out. By November 1953 Cvetic was denouncing Sherman as "unreliable, irresponsible, and at times flagrantly untruthful." Musmanno and Cvetic remained friends until the latter's death in 1962.[29]

They came from similar immigrant backgrounds. Both of Musmanno's parents had emigrated from Italy to the United States. The family for a long time was known as Musmann, according to an FBI report, because "when [the] father first came to this country, one of his employers erroneously entered his name on the payroll records, and . . . [the] father became known by this name." Musmanno was born in 1897 in a small semirural township on the Ohio River some six miles from Pittsburgh. He had eight siblings who survived infancy (four brothers, one of whom died in action during World War I, and four sisters). As he later put it, "I was by no means a child of fortune." The father scrabbled for a living as a coal miner, as a railroad section hand, and for a brief time as a local police constable. Musmanno recalls beginning at age fourteen "remunerative employment . . . as a loader in a coal mine" and having to "attend school at night." His post–high school education was interrupted by brief military service during World War I. Aggressively ambitious he had a great love of learning and earned various academic degrees while employed at odd jobs. An almost incredulous FBI man later reported: Musmanno "was awarded an LL.B. degree from Georgetown University Law School . . . in 1918; in 1919 he enrolled at George Washington University and was awarded an A.B. degree in 1921 and an M.A. in 1922 . . . , the National University Law School, Washington, DC awarded him the Master of Laws . . . in June 1923.

He also attended American University . . . at the same time . . . and
. . . was awarded the degree . . . Doctor of Jurisprudence by the . . .
University in June of 1923."[30]

Admitted to the Pennsylvania bar during the summer of
1923, Musmanno despite his multiple degrees found that in
Philadelphia the established firms demanded something else. "It almost seemed," he recalled, "that one had to be born into those offices or enter through an old men's home." He finally managed to
catch on with a general practice firm and litigated over sixty low-
level cases, many of them dealing with criminal law. Notwithstanding a very positive trial record, a disenchanted Musmanno struck out
for Europe, spending most of his time abroad in Italy. There at the
University of Rome he relatively quickly earned the Dottore di
Giurisprudenze degree. He recalled supporting himself at part-time
jobs, including a stint as an extra in the movie epic *Ben Hur,* then
being filmed by an American company on the outskirts of Rome.[31]

Musmanno's Communist adversaries, especially Nelson,
made much of his study in Fascist Italy and of a 1926 letter to the editor published by the *Pittsburgh Press* commending a "heroic Mussolini" and the Fascisti for accepting "the full moral, historical, and
political responsibility for . . . driving Bolshevism from the country."
Musmanno was not alone in his admiration at this time for the Fascist dictator. Lincoln Steffens, a pivotal figure in American radical-
ism, compared Mussolini favorably to Theodore Roosevelt in 1927.
One of Steffens's biographers has well summed up the response to
the Italian leader in the 1920s: "For . . . intellectuals and businessmen alike, readers of the *New Republic* as well as the *Saturday Evening
Post* . . . Mussolini . . . stood out as a typical hero of the times, the
supreme pragmatist and achiever." The FBI found that after Musmanno's return from Rome in 1925 that "he changed his name to
Musmanno, claiming that this was the correct family name."[32]

Over the next few years he had some success as an attorney
in Pittsburgh, especially in personal damage cases. He was a vigorous tenacious advocate in pursuit of his clients' rights, and became
known as "a champion of the underprivileged." He took time out in
1927 from his practice to serve with the Sacco and Vanzetti defense
team during the last months of the long unsuccessful campaign to

spare their lives and to rectify the legal injustices done to the two men. Musmanno had run as a Republican for the lower house of the Pennsylvania General Assembly in 1926 and lost. Again a GOP candidate in 1928 he won by a narrow margin, becoming the youngest member to that date elected to serve in that house. He was reelected by a much wider margin in 1930. During his terms in the legislature Musmanno pushed diverse proposals, including a Barbers' License Bill, which passed as a health measure. He failed in attempts to end imprisonment for civil debt and to ameliorate the state's notorious "blue laws" that forbade such activities as "baseball, movies, and musical concerts" on Sunday (he was especially outraged that "of course those wealthy enough to belong to private clubs could snap their fingers at the blue laws").[33]

Musmanno also failed despite yeoman efforts to have passed legislation that would effectively control or abolish Pennsylvania's notorious "Coal and Iron Police." A private force invested with sovereign police power and used by the state's "barons of industry" ostensibly to protect their property, in reality the Coal and Iron Police ruthlessly squelched any attempts at union organization. Composed in the main of what Musmanno called "society's outcasts," they had a record of brutality and violation of individual rights. In February 1929 two members of the Coal and Iron Police beat a miner named John Barcolski to death in their barracks. Even after Barcolski—innocent of any wrongdoing whatsoever—died, the two Coal and Iron Police "continued the fusillade of blows with whip, poker, knuckles, revolver butt, and thong." Musmanno preserved Barcolski's memory by writing "Jan Volkanik," a story later incorporated into a 1935 Warner Brothers movie, *Black Fury,* starring Paul Muni. Musmanno toured Pennsylvania with the film urging "repeal of the police laws" and later credited the critically well-received film with doing much to accomplish that goal. His spirited attack during the 1930s on the Coal and Iron Police, well-remembered, blunted much of the Communist attack on him when he red-baited them in the early 1950s.[34]

In the late 1920s and early 1930s the Pennsylvania legislature convened only every other year and generally only for half a week during the four to six months that the legislators met. Musmanno thus had the time available to develop what he described as "a rather good law practice." In 1931 he was elected to the Allegheny County Court, and two years later won a ten-year term on the Common Pleas Court, taking 94 percent of the vote cast. An activist judge known to favor labor, he clashed periodically with his more conservative colleagues. A shrewd publicity seeker, Musmanno crusaded against drunk drivers. He held court at night in order to dispose of such cases, held court in a morgue to which had been sent the bodies of the victims of drunk drivers, and meted out over four hundred jail sentences for driving while intoxicated. He seems to have been very effective: one newspaper credited him with "a 65% decrease in drunken driving in Pittsburgh." He also seems as a result of his crackdown to have angered the Chief Judge, whose son represented defendants in various cases, which according to one report "included some political and influential personages." His mostly Republican peers took umbrage at the fact that he "adjourned court" for the day in January 1937 on which President Roosevelt's second inauguration took place.[35]

In 1938 the Roosevelt administration considered Musmanno for an appointment to the Third Circuit Court of Appeals (the Appeals Courts have been described as "the last legal step" before the Supreme Court). The Third Circuit then covered Pennsylvania, Delaware, and New Jersey. As usual in the consideration of such appointments, the Attorney General asked the FBI to vet the possible candidate. However because of Musmanno's attack on "law enforcement" in the person of the Coal and Iron Police, Hoover does not seem to have much cared for him. However, Hoover did not need to interject himself, given what his agents were told. The Bureau cast its net wide in soliciting information about Musmanno and found that while some praised him many faulted him for being a publicity seeker. They criticized him for lacking "the delicate sense and poise which all judges should have," for conducting court in "the manner of a 'Barnum & Bailey' circus." They maintained that "the local bar association" could certainly find someone "more suitable," that "it would be a grave mistake to appoint a man of the caliber and reputation" of Musmanno, who it was said disparagingly "wore a flowing black tie" and "his hair long."[36]

Although the press considered the "liberal" Musmanno a fit "Roosevelt appointment to a court that has never upheld the National Labor Relations Board," the administration decided on a less controversial candidate. In 1943, he was reelected to another ten-year term on the Common Pleas Court. But he ran in absentia, since in 1942 he had joined the Navy and left to fight in World War II.[37]

Six years elapsed before he returned to Pittsburgh in late 1948 to take the judicial oath of office. Between 1942 and 1945 he rose from lieutenant commander to captain (he ultimately retired from the U.S. Naval Reserve as a rear admiral). While on convoy duty, he suffered the sinking of his ship by German planes. He participated in the 1943 Allied invasion of Italy, served as Naval Aide to General Mark Clark—commander of the U.S. Fifth Army, which did much of the fighting on the Italian front, and served for six months as military governor of the Sorrentine Peninsula by the Bay of Naples. His many decorations included the Purple Heart (with cluster) and the Bronze Star. In 1946, while Clark was U.S. High Commissioner for occupied Austria, Musmanno became head of a board of forcible repatriation. As strongly anti-Communist as ever, Musmanno (in the words of one biographer) "was able to prevent many refugees from being returned to their Communist-dominated homelands."[38]

Appointed a judge for the lesser trials of Nazi war criminals, he participated in three tribunals, presiding over the Einsatzgruppen case—termed by the Associated Press as "the biggest murder trial in history." The Einsatzgruppen were "special task forces" sent to Eastern Europe to kill people the Nazis considered inferior. The twenty-two defendants were high-ranking SS officials charged with more than a million deaths. An American translator at the trial noted that "at no time did any defendant express remorse for his actions." Musmanno's three-judge court sentenced fourteen of the defendants to death; however, because of changing international circumstances—West Germany had become increasingly important to the United States—many of these sentences were commuted by the U.S. High Commission for Germany. Earlier Musmanno had worked with a team investigating Hitler's death. Musmanno's 1950 account of Hitler's last days, *Ten Days to Die*, later was filmed in Austria as *Der Letze Akt* (The last act). Both book and film met an indifferent critical reception. In 1961 as a result of these experiences and at the behest of Israeli authorities Musmanno served as a prosecution witness in their trial of Adolf Eichmann, who had overseen and facilitated much of "the Final Solution," and who had been whisked to Israel from his Argentinean refuge by Nazi hunters. Musmanno testified out of a sense of "impelling duty" and strongly defended Israel's right to try Eichmann.[39]

In 1950 he ran on the Democratic Party's losing ticket for lieutenant governor of Pennsylvania. The next year with a good margin statewide he was elected to a twenty-one-year term on Pennsylvania's highest court, becoming "its first member of Italian descent." Thirteen years later, in 1964, came his "last hurrah" in electoral politics; by a few hundred votes he lost a bitter, very hard fought primary for the Democratic nomination for U.S. Senator. Musmanno continued, as an obituary pointed out, "to champion the underprivileged and the oppressed." He never lost his passion or vigor but in his final years he also turned somewhat eccentric. In 1965 the Yale University Press published a book arguing for the validity of a map that authenticated the Vikings as reaching America nearly five hundred years before Columbus. Then as now "the Vinland Map" remains controversial (in 1996 the Smithsonian's Wilcomb Washburn said "nothing puts the controversy to rest"). Musmanno after 1965 had helped keep it alive. There always had been references, for example, in U.S. history books to the Vikings; nearly a century earlier William Cullen Bryant and Sydney Howard Gay had speculated about the landfall of the Norsemen and suggested "Nantucket," among other places. Musmanno always fervently proud of his Italian heritage, sprang into action devoting "enormous energy and endless rhetoric" (as one Pittsburgh newspaper put it) insisting "Columbus WAS first." He did so in a 1966 book, as well as in the words of one newsman "haranguing the public . . . with his insistence that Columbus not the Vikings discovered America."[40]

Fittingly Musmanno died on Columbus Day 1968. Per his request burial was in Arlington National Cemetery "in a plot as close as reasonably possible to that occupied by our beloved President John F. Kennedy." After his death the Pittsburgh newspapers paid tribute to him for his "energy," his "passion," his "war record," his battle to "rid Pennsylvania of its hated iron and coal police," and his "participation in the defense of Sacco and Vanzetti." The last involved Musmanno with the International Labor Defense, an organization that in time made its way to the Attorney General's List. The 1948 FBI memo that reported this involvement with a "subversive organization" also noted that "reliable confidential informant(s) . . . state that Judge Musmanno has never been engaged in Communist activities." Shortly thereafter, aided and abetted by Cvetic, Musmanno became very engaged in anti-Communist activities.[41]

Musmanno, unlike many others, never turned his back on Cvetic and remained responsive to him long after the informant was well away from the limelight. However, their initially symbiotic relationship fairly quickly devolved into one in which Cvetic was a very junior partner but remained so "wholeheartedly." The opening salvo in their joint attack on Communism and Communists in Pennsylvania came in early March 1950 when Cvetic identified a potential Pittsburgh grand juror as a CP member. At Musmanno's summons Cvetic, while still under subpoena to HUAC, flew from Washington to Pittsburgh and confronted the juror, Alice Roth, in the judge's chambers; she called Cvetic "a rat" (more than once); the judge threw her off the panel; Cvetic flew back to HUAC. Some weeks later the press reported that a higher state court had dismissed her appeal "because she was the 24th person called for duty—23 is the legal limit," but rebuked the judge.[42]

During Musmanno's 1950 campaign for lieutenant governor he highlighted his anti-Communism, always referencing as his source "undercover FBI agent Matt Cvetic," who was often found standing alongside the judge in what now are called "photo opportunities." In late August 1950 Musmanno, on the basis of a little-known and possibly never used 1919 state sedition law, swore out a "criminal information" warrant against Nelson and two other Communist leaders. Cvetic participated in the August 31 raid led by Musmanno on CP headquarters in Pittsburgh. Musmanno probably acted legally but certainly overdramatically. Accompanied by some city detectives and a mob of photographers and reporters, Musmanno and Cvetic, in the words of one accompanying journalist, "gave the down-at-the-heels Communist offices a fast once over, selecting at random several arms full of subversive literature to be used as evidence."[43]

Cvetic testified against Nelson at the ensuing trial of Pennsylvania CP leaders in April 1951. After an auto accident Nelson was severed from that long-running trial, which had begun in January 1951 and did not end until eight months later. At the end of August 1951 the remaining two defendants were unsurprisingly found guilty. In January 1952 Cvetic testified at Nelson's second trial for sedition, which ran from December 1951 to June 1952. Cvetic did not fare well on the stand in either trial. In the second one he proved unable to deal with Nelson, who acted as his own attorney (and as Musmanno later ruefully admitted "handled himself rather well"). An angry Nelson, who had been "just waiting to cross-examine" his former comrade, pounded away at Cvetic with a withering barrage of questions while referring to him as a "fingerman" and a "professional patriot."[44]

In these trials as in the few others in which he served as a witness Cvetic performed poorly. He had a certain shrewd native glibness, which could sustain him when faced at House and Senate Committee hearings with the usual friendly queries. Otherwise he needed help. In 1951 (probably at Musmanno's instigation, although the judge denied involvement) Cvetic filed a sedition charge against Hyman Schlesinger, described as "long-term counsel for Communists in western Pennsylvania." Although the initiator of the charge, Cvetic depended on Sherman to carry it through. At an extremely contentious June 1951 hearing marked by much name-calling, Sherman called Schlesinger's lawyer "Mr. Communist," that lawyer called Cvetic "a witness for sale," and so on. Cvetic testified about Schlesinger under Sherman's leading questions. Schlesinger's counsel attacked Cvetic and Sherman. While Sherman held his own, "a perspiring, chain-smoking" Cvetic refused to answer some questions put to him as Sherman's objections were overruled.[45]

In December 1951 the sedition charges were quashed. But Cvetic had intruded on Schlesinger's life and would continue to do so for another decade. Schlesinger had to wage a long hard fight against disbarment for "professional misconduct" based on Cvetic's statements about the lawyer's alleged CP membership and close involvement in Party affairs. In 1960 Schlesinger was disbarred. The next year Pennsylvania's highest court settled the matter once and for all, ruling, among other things, that "the Bar Association had acted improperly as prosecutor, judge, and jury" and that "the Bar Association did not explain how Mr. Schlesinger had violated the oath he took on admission to the Bar." [46]

Cvetic could not stand up to a hostile grilling in court. He did not think quickly and often hesitated while being cross-examined. At one point during his February 1951 testimony at the IWO trial, one of the organization's lawyers said, "Your Honor, I should like the record to indicate the long pause in which the witness is trying to, let us say, frame his answer to this question." During the first Nelson trial one newspaper reported that Cvetic so took his time in responding to a question that the Communists' attorney "snapped, 'well, why don't you answer?'" During the IWO trial, being questioned about his veracity, Cvetic said, "I approximate the answer on the best basis of the testimony I am giving at the time." And sometimes to the dismay of the prosecutors utilizing Cvetic, he would not even "approximate" an answer to opposing counsel, but rather simply retreat (successfully) behind unresponsive statements, as he did at the first Nelson trial where in response to a question he said, "I don't want the Communist conspiracy to know as much as the FBI does." [47]

After his 1951 court appearances he served as a government witness at only one more major trial. He continued to appear until 1955 at congressional hearings. But most of all he served the U.S. Immigration and Naturalization Service (INS) as a witness at numerous denaturalization and deportation hearings. Right after Cvetic surfaced, the INS had queried the FBI whether "it had any objections . . . toward utilizing his services." And newsman Taylor reported on March 1, 1950, just after Cvetic finished his first round of HUAC hearings that "Cvetic may help to deport some ex-'Comrades.'" [48]

Cvetic had a dark side. It would take some time for it to become apparent publicly. From the moment he surfaced, for nearly half a decade Cvetic was a media darling. Even his stumbling performances during court proceedings did not generally become known for some time. Whatever was said on the fringes by the *Daily Worker* or by journalist I. F. Stone (who wondered in print how it had come to pass that Cvetic "was graduating from undercover agent to public hero") went for naught. The media had created a "Cvetic" and for a few years more some in the business continued to peddle that creation.[49]

four

The Media

The mass media of the time "made" Cvetic—and not just in Pittsburgh. Cvetic benefited from the media savvy of those who promoted him, both his initial sponsors and those who came along later. When in time he wore out his usefulness and had to act on his own, Cvetic found the going rough. He could no longer convincingly sell the image that his promoters had created or cover up his previous shortcomings. Americans Battling Communism got the mythic ball rolling in Pittsburgh. Having its own agenda, the organization did not tie Cvetic up contractually. Before he began his March 1950 HUAC testimony, Cvetic signed an agreement with Sherman and Moore allotting each of them 30 percent of the "new proceeds of any undertaking that resulted from the promotion or sale of the Cvetic story." Sherman as "attorney-agent" and Moore as "author-editor" promised in return, among other things, "to the best" of their abilities to promote "the Cvetic story."[1]

This they did. Sherman, until January 1952, when he broke with Cvetic, appeared with him before HUAC as his counsel and with him at most public engagements, such as the UE rallies. Sherman, whose break with Cvetic did not immediately become public, later claimed, without exaggeration, that he "sponsored," "tutored," and "trained" Cvetic. During the weeks following Cvetic's February and March 1950 HUAC testimony, Sherman and Moore took advantage of the enormous favorable national media coverage that Cvetic had garnered. They pursued various deals. One that particularly annoyed the FBI was the deal with the NBC program *We, the People,* which had been a feature on radio for twelve years before moving to TV in 1948–it was the first regularly scheduled series to be simulcast on both network radio and network television.[2]

Essentially a half-hour interview show, its format called for the host (Dan Seymour) to interview both famous and ordinary people. Each show had more than one segment. On July 14, 1950, Seymour introduced "the story of a double life . . . the story of great heroism, of terror, of an incredible nine-year span of daily suspense that you will now hear from Gulf Oil's next guest, Matt Cvetic." Like all guests on the program Cvetic was introduced with the tag line "we, the people . . . speak." A modest-sounding Cvetic opened with the lines: "Don't call this a hero's story. It's not. It's just the story of an ordinary guy named Matt Cvetic . . . who was asked to do a tough job by his country. A guy who was scared–but a guy who couldn't say no."[3]

In a series of reenactments an actor portrayed Cvetic with his FBI "contact," with (as the TV script put it) a "Video Mama Type, holding dish towel, dish, very troubled," asking "in a slight accent" the actor portraying Cvetic "Why, Mattie? Why? You are strange man . . . a big Communist," and with a group of suspicious Communists "staring down at him" as Seymour talks about "a close call." The program overall followed the same song of sacrifice that Cvetic had sung for weeks, including an inspiring Father Lawless referring to the religious devotion Cvetic's undercover work forced him to eschew. Lawless reported that when "Matt was afraid or lonely, he would come at night to the side door of the rectory" and "alone with me, he would pray."[4]

The Bureau did not pass judgment on the program's presentation of Cvetic but did express concern and irritation about unveiling the correct name of an agent on the air and about the fact that this one-time FBI agent–William B. Mooney–"former supervisor for western Pennsylvania–Northern Virginia" was presented as Cvetic's initial Pittsburgh Bureau "contact." Mooney appeared briefly before being replaced by an actor who took up the narrative. The Pittsburgh Bureau reported to the Director that Mooney was not the initial contact; he "was . . . working in the Milwaukee Office" when

Cvetic joined up and was not "transferred to Pittsburgh until August of 1944." Later, during the IWO trial Cvetic himself admitted that Mooney, who had retired to Waverly, Iowa, "wasn't the original contact man." Thus, as he had done before and was to do again with so many other aspects of his story, Cvetic had bent the truth.[5]

The FBI, after due consideration of the Cvetic segment of *We, the People,* concluded "it does not appear that there is any desirable action that can be taken with regard to the manner in which Cvetic's story was presented." The day after the Bureau reached this conclusion, one of Hoover's chief assistants reported that "it appears that Cvetic has now taken to drink." The FBI's concern about how the media would present Cvetic, his foibles, and his relationship to the Bureau increased as media interest in him grew.[6]

The *We, the People* broadcast took place almost simultaneously with the publication in the *Saturday Evening Post* of the first of three installments in which Cvetic, "as told to Pete Martin," described how "I Posed as a Communist for the FBI." The *Post* at that time had "a unique place in the heart of Middle America" (to use the words of one magazine history). Probably for that reason, during the Cold War years the *Post* was a favorite vehicle for the stories of recanters, defectors, and government types peddling mainstream anti-Communism. Such stories, along with lively celebrity articles such as "Pete Martin Calls On" or his "as told to," were part of the editorial mix that enabled the *Post* at that time (as journalist Theodore White recalls) to maintain itself as "one of the big four of the newsstands," alongside such magazines as *Life* and *Look.* Moore knew William Thornton "Pete" Martin, then a *Post* associate editor. Competent, productive, concerned—Martin had to be convinced that working with Cvetic would be worthwhile. Moore apparently clinched the deal by sending Martin a scrapbook of Cvetic's press clippings. On March 20, 1950, Cvetic—as well as Moore and Sherman—signed a contract with the *Saturday Evening Post,* which bought the rights to "the story" for $5,000; only $1,000 of which was paid on signing.[7]

The *Post* articles once more presented a self-sacrificing, patriotically driven Cvetic, a man different from the informant known to his Bureau contacts. The Washington FBI reviewers of the articles found nothing disturbing in any of them. There was some dissatisfaction—a bemoaning of the exposure of the Bureau technique of "replacing lights with bulbs of more powerful wattage" in order to facilitate filming nighttime Communist meetings, and an expression of annoyance at the "innuendo" that Cvetic had been involved with the Bureau bugging of a Pittsburgh CP meeting room—an action involving George Dietze, about which Cvetic had no knowledge at the time. Overall the FBI reviewers found "all references to the FBI were laudatory," and that the articles generally placed the Bureau "in a good light by the manner in which it utilized the services of . . . Cvetic."[8]

In legal proceedings over the coming years those individuals attacking Cvetic's credibility made much of his admissions that the articles were only "substantially true," that they used "Pete Martin's words, not mine," that "I supplied some of the data for it; Harry Sherman supplied some; Jim Moore supplied some; Pete wrote the article, and there were even . . . several rewrite men working on it." Nelson, serving as his own attorney in the second Pennsylvania sedition trial, caught Cvetic in contradictions between the article, other public utterances, and the HUAC testimony and asked him, "Do you tailor your testimony to fit the needs . . . Mr. Witness?" Cvetic's plays for sympathy in the article, for example, his fanciful tales about his mother's plea to leave the Party and spare the family name, were distortions, but much of what Cvetic said about the CP and Communists holds up. As with his February and March HUAC testimony (whether coached or not) the articles have a basis in reality—if only because they identify Party members and fronts; however, to repeat what Nelson later pointed out, in 1950 Cvetic "named names already publicly known."[9]

Cvetic's behavior did ultimately descend to the contemptible, but many of his most vociferous critics had their own shortcomings. The critic Richard Schickel in another context has put it well: "There's a naivete about American Communism as if they were just a bit more liberal . . . which is just not true." Whatever Cvetic became, the Communist leaders of the 1940s and early 1950s do not wear particularly well—a judgment that is, as the writer Robert Conquest puts it, "overwhelmingly a matter of factual investigations and deduction . . . the discovery of the real." Moreover, as subsequent revelations have shown, much of what Cvetic said initially has proved true. He did quite rapidly destroy his credibility as a witness but he did so for reasons other than the content of these articles.[10]

As to the *Post* articles, Cvetic and his associates can be faulted for either not understanding the editorial process or failing to pay close attention to it. Cvetic once quite incredulously said, "They write and rewrite . . . at least a dozen people work on these articles before they are actually published." Cvetic and his associates did not really review what Martin wrote and what the *Post* planned to publish. It is possible that Cvetic was simply too lazy to read the galleys. It is probable that Sherman and Moore were otherwise preoccupied, especially since Cvetic was not proving to be the anticipated cash cow. Obviously, as far as the *Post* was concerned, there were problems with the Cvetic story—four articles had been planned, but only three appeared.[11]

The transcripts of the thirteen Dicta-belts of conversations which Martin held with Cvetic and used as a basis by the writer for his articles adhere fairly closely to the February and June 1950 HUAC testimony on the CP, its members, and Communist fronts. These transcripts, however, also include the sentimental guff Cvetic told HUAC, so emphasized by *We, the People*. If in general the *Post* articles held to reality, in some details they played down events inconvenient to the Cvetic myth and ignored his drinking, his firing by the FBI, and the shortcomings touched on by the Bureau in its review of what the *Post* had published. The articles emphasized the ugly picture of Communism in America drawn in the latter 1940s by defectors, informers, recanters, and surfacing undercover operatives—in short, to use the words of historian Lee Adler, as "a secret conspiratorial movement in the interests of a foreign power (i.e., the Soviet Union)." Whatever the reality of this view, and however much the *Post* articles did contribute to it, the personal story of Cvetic's sacrifice and devotion Martin laid out was a fabrication. The *Post* articles built on earlier manifestations of that fabrication. The movie version of Cvetic's story would further exaggerate that fabrication, almost beyond belief.[12]

Motion picture studios, including Warner Brothers, had expressed an interest in Cvetic's story even before the *Post* articles appeared. In August 1950, Warner Brothers bought the rights to Cvetic's story as set forth in the *Post* for $12,500. The studio agreed to pay $3,125 on execution of the contracts, $3,125 on November 5, 1950, and $6,250 on March 5, 1951. Cvetic certainly seemed to have recovered from the economic problems he had faced a few months earlier. But in the end, he did not fare well financially. Even in 1950 terms, Warner Brothers laid out little for the rights: consider the $75,000 Twentieth Century-Fox paid the Soviet defector Igor Gouzenko for the rights to his story.[13]

As with the *Post* series, a number of people had "a part of the action." Cvetic had to share the money paid out by the film studio because, as the movie contract correctly pointed out, "Moore and . . . Sherman have . . . assisted Cvetic in publishing said experiences." Cvetic had to share the money Warner Brothers paid, and not just with Sherman and Moore. The *Post* contract required that Martin receive 15 percent of whatever the film rights brought. According to Sherman, Cvetic retained only 40 percent of the proceeds from the movie sale. Nor did Cvetic enjoy fringe benefits such as Martin wrangled from the studio. Warner Brothers engaged the *Post* editor for two weeks as a "consultant and adviser" on the Cvetic project, paying Martin $500 weekly, plus $200 in living expenses as well as the cost of travel back and forth across the country. The studio also assured Martin that while in California "you will have a reasonable amount of time to carry out your regular . . . Post interviewing assignments."[14]

Warner Brothers, more than any previous entity involved with developing "the Cvetic story," distorted Cvetic's activities and life. The studio, which had no interest in making a didactic film, added melodramatic fictions designed to make the movie more commercial. These distortions did not become evident in the studio's statements during preproduction, even though once Warner Brothers became involved, its publicity machine went to work. A plethora of stories appeared announcing the studio's intent to make a "quality" film "in the documentary style." Studio press releases described the project as "a film in the traditions of *Confessions of a Nazi Spy,*" a serious and well-received 1939 Warner Brothers production that was among Hollywood's earliest overtly anti-Nazi films. Jack Warner, the studio's head of production (or his public relations "ghost"), grandly declared, "It is my hope that with this picture Warner Brothers will be able to halt the march of those who are trying to undermine the foundations of our democratic structure" and asserted that Cvetic deserved "a decoration for civilian heroism." [15]

Even in an industry given to hyperbole, Jack Warner obviously exaggerated, but like the production executives at other Hollywood studios, he sought a genre that would halt the erosion of the moviegoing audience. That audience reached a peak in 1946 and began declining in 1947, long before most American cities had television. The increasing impact of television in the later 1940s only hastened the decline. Various factors played a role in declining movie attendance, including changing demographics (the postwar move to the suburbs, which removed the potential audience from the downtown theaters), and increasing competition for the average American's "leisure dollar" (e.g., from organized sports as well as activities such as golf and interior decorating).[16]

The economic problems arising from the declining audience were further compounded by the court decisions that forced the movie industry to choose formally between production and exhibition. The culmination of the Justice Department's antitrust actions against Hollywood for over a decade came in mid-1949 with a final ruling that "separation of the studios from exhibition was a necessary remedy." The forced sale of their theaters subsequently reduced the profitability of the studios: the Warner Brothers theaters, for example, before being sold, had earned 62 percent of that corporation's profits. The studios sought a new genre in order to recapture the movie audience, and also determined to make use of their old formulas in a more up-to-date fashion. Thus anti-Communism replaced the anti-Fascism of World War II. The studios also obviously hoped to placate those who charged the studios with pro-Communist output. But *I Was a Communist for the FBI* was an investment more than a political sop. It was conceived and filmed well after the 1947 HUAC hearing on the industry and months before a new series of investigations by HUAC. Warner Brothers sought to use the old formulas, updated to the Cold War, but failed to understand the changes that had taken place in the audience. The studio's approach to the Cvetic story underscores French director/critic François Truffaut's observation that a film "becomes a sociological event and the question of quality becomes secondary." [17]

Notwithstanding the studio's stated commitment to "quality," when in August 1950 Warner Brothers announced purchase of "the Cvetic Story," the choice of production personnel indicated otherwise. The producer, Bryan Foy, had a reputation stretching back into the 1920s for churning out melodramas cheaply and quickly. He had gained renown at various studios, in one critic's words, "for endlessly reusing the same story in different guises." Foy proudly recalled having utilized one plot in five different movies, the settings ranging from a circus to the Northwest woods. Known for his "loyalty to old friends," Foy tapped one of them, Crane Wilbur, to fashion Cvetic's story for the screen. Wilbur's career as an actor, director, and writer began in the theater before World War I. He made his screen debut in 1914 opposite serial queen Pearl White in *The Perils of Pauline*. As a writer, melodrama was his forte, but not always successfully; for example, a New York critic began a review of a Wilbur play by "apologizing to the virgin paper for having to soil it" by writing about the play. Wilbur ventured to Hollywood in the 1930s as a writer and director and worked mostly on B-film melodramas. [18]

When Wilbur left the Cvetic project for a time, he was succeeded by Bordon Chase, who had pronounced conservative political views. However, Chase was assigned to the Cvetic story not for that reason but because of his availability and successful record of action-oriented screenplays. Born Frank Fowler in Brooklyn, Chase after several careers had come to Hollywood in the 1940s and worked at various studios. His output included "B" programmers as well as *Red River*, a 1948 western (described as "a classic of the genre") which had earned him an Academy Award nomination. The director of the Cvetic film, Gordon Douglas, in the words of one writer, held "no illusions about himself." He told an interviewer: "I guess some people would say I was a whore . . . but I would rather work." Described by critic Andrew Sarris as an "efficient technician," for over a decade the forty-one-year-old Douglas had without particular distinction directed comedies, mysteries, and swashbucklers, as well as one of the first anti-Communist movies, *Walk a*

Crooked Mile (a 1948 release in which the FBI and Scotland Yard teamed up to catch a gang of Communist spies). To Douglas it, like the Cvetic film, was just another assignment.[19]

At one point Kirk Douglas and Ruth Roman, then rising stars, were considered for the roles of Cvetic and the "girl" created for the film's story. However, as Cvetic the studio cast Frank Lovejoy, a former radio actor who was a solid but undistinguished contract player used for leads in lesser films such as this and in supporting roles in more important features. The part of the girl went to Dorothy Hart, an attractive but undistinguished contract player; this was one of her last film roles. James Millican, a utility actor in numerous action films, played the Nelson character. Warner contract actors Philip Carey and Richard Webb, both of whom later carved out careers on television (the latter as "Captain Midnight"), played Cvetic's FBI contacts.[20]

Wilbur finished his treatment in September 1950 before moving on to another project. His version of Cvetic's story added a "sincere" romance as well as gangster film elements such as two CP-ordered murders disguised as suicides. Wilbur followed closely some of the details Cvetic had related to Pete Martin—as can be seen from the passages the screenwriter marked in the *Post* editor's 102-page transcript of his conversations with Cvetic (not all of which material appeared in the articles). Incidents related to Martin but not used by him found their way into Wilbur's forty-six-page treatment. The screen writer, like *We, the People* and Martin, parroted Cvetic's fabrications about his CP activities, his sacrifices, his problems with his family, his fears about exposure and retribution, and his views on Nelson and other CP leaders.[21]

Chase began work in October 1950. An industrious and speedy writer, by December 9, 1950, he had turned in another treatment as well as two scripts and some "revised pages." He then moved on to another assignment. Chase made little use of Martin's transcript of his conversations with Cvetic or of the Wilbur treatment. All the versions written by Chase reeked of simple-minded anti-Communism, melodramatic coincidence, and "B" gangster-film conventions. Indeed, someone at Warner who read Chase's first effort wrote on its cover the admonition "tell as 92nd St." This note referred to a well-received 1945 Twentieth Century–Fox film, *The House on 92nd Street,* which in straightforward, documentarylike fashion detailed the FBI roundup of a gang of Nazi spies. None of Chase's versions had any of that film's restraint.[22]

The problem of delineating the Steve Nelson character epitomizes the script problems faced by Chase and the studio. Foy and others at Warner could not decide on just how to portray Nelson, but whatever the script he always remained a threat to Cvetic. In one draft Nelson clearly gives the orders—be it for espionage, murder, or merely cutting off a long-winded speaker at an American Slav Congress meeting. In another draft Nelson, now called Beldon, became a senior underling fearful of his superiors in New York City and Moscow—so much so that Cvetic could successfully parry the Nelson character by warning "Knock me off and you'll be the next to go."[23]

The continuing script problems resulted in a lessening of studio interest and the elimination of scenes that might cost more to film. All the versions scripted by Chase drew on the contemporary American media's red-baiting view of domestic and international Communism and glorified Cvetic and the FBI. Before Chase moved on, the studio determined to change the film's title. "I Posed as a Communist for the FBI" (the title of the Cvetic-Martin *Post* articles) became *I Was a Communist for the FBI.* Such a change in title was not unusual in Hollywood, but in this instance the change also reflected Warner Brothers' serious problems in coming to grips with Cvetic's story as presented in the *Saturday Evening Post.*[24]

Wilbur, having finished his other chores for the studio, returned to the project during the second week of December 1950. The incomplete script Wilbur turned in just before Christmas found little favor with studio executives. The script had little to do with his previous efforts or Chase's various versions. On December 30 Wilbur turned in the first part of yet another revised script blending his earlier efforts with Chase's versions and adding some new touches. Anxious studio executives decided to shoot this version even though Wilbur essentially had produced a "B" melodrama with some limited and very unsophisticated red-baiting ideological overtones.[25]

Production began on January 6, 1951. By that date Wilbur

had completed about 45 percent of the script. While production rolled on, he finished the screenplay. At the same time, responding to suggestions from Foy and Douglas, he revised pages of script turned in earlier, often just a few days before. The revisions further cheapened the ideological content and heightened the melodrama. Wilbur completed the bulk of his work by February 5, but principal photography continued until February 21. The film's original schedule had called for twenty-four days of shooting, an additional sixteen days more were needed despite Douglas's use of Saturdays and evenings.[26]

In Hollywood, studios often tinker with their films after the completion of principal photography to make them better box-office. *I Was a Communist for the FBI* was no exception. Studio executives, unsure of how to present the Cvetic story attractively on screen, tried to fine-tune the film. They got little assistance from Cvetic, ostensibly a "technical adviser." According to FBI reports, he exploited his newfound celebrity with one-night lecture stands in Pittsburgh and its environs, appearing at local Kiwanis and Lions Clubs as well as American Legion posts, between severe alcoholic binges (one of which landed him in a Pittsburgh jail). To the surprise and dismay of Warner Brothers personnel, the FBI—usually among the most cooperative of government agencies—made it clear that in regard to Cvetic and the movie "it was too late to give any advice" and that the filmmakers "could do what they wished." Indeed, Hoover's office sent a memo to all local FBI branches announcing that "the Bureau did not approve this picture" and instructing all agency personnel to respond "tactfully" to inquiries about the film with the statement that the FBI "had absolutely nothing to do with its production." The lack of FBI cooperation was felt at every level: a Pittsburgh public relations man for Warner Brothers recalled years later how inexplicable it seemed to him at the time that he "couldn't get any assistance from the usually cooperative local FBI agents."[27]

The studio's tinkering continued almost to the world premiere, which took place in Pittsburgh on April 19, 1951. Three weeks earlier Warner Brothers reshot one of the final scenes between Cvetic and his son. On April 14, just hours before release, when prints were being prepared for shipment across the country, the studio hurriedly arranged for the processing laboratory to cut some twenty-two feet from the film. As a result of "bad reactions" at press previews, the studio cut the following lines spoken by Cvetic about the Soviet Union: "Their state capitalism is a Fascist horror far worse than anything Hitler ever intended for the world. That great liar of all times spoke the truth when he warned that to the East there was an enemy even more dangerous than he." Such absurdities dominated the shooting script that Wilbur had cobbled together from his own earlier efforts and those of Chase.[28]

The studio did not film all Wilbur's red-baiting flights of fancy. Eliminated from production, for example, was part of a scene during which one of a team of Party goons assigned to work Cvetic over shouts at him, "Our system makes Murder Incorporated look like an amateur setup." But a great many Cold War clichés found their way into the finished film. Cvetic on screen sermonizes directly at the audience during his HUAC testimony in words that went far beyond anything he said during his 1950 appearances before that congressional committee: the American Communist Party, the film Cvetic warns, "is actually a vast spy system founded in this country by the Soviet Union, and composed of American traitors whose only purpose is to deliver the people of the United States into the hands of Russia as a colony of slaves." The Nelson character, now called James Blandon, informs his associates that "sometimes a Communist must turn his coat for the good of the cause. Didn't Comrade Stalin join with Hitler in '39?" At a reception for a visiting Party dignitary, the Pittsburgh CP leadership led by Blandon all toast Stalin.[29]

The movie outraged Nelson, especially the portrayal of Blandon—and with good reason. *I Was a Communist for the FBI* presented Blandon as a hypocritical, racist, murderous, swinish Moscow flunky (just the media image of your average everyday American CP leader in the early 1950s). The movie had its world premiere in Pittsburgh during Nelson's first sedition trial, just before the auto accident that caused his severance from the case. Nelson argued, and not without justification, during his second trial that because of the movie his chances of getting a fair jury trial in Pittsburgh had become even more unlikely. He argued that whatever name Warner Brothers gave to the movie's CP Pittsburgh head, any jury would assume that Nelson had committed the foul deeds depicted on the screen. Nelson never denied being a Communist, but always declared that Cvetic, on the witness stand and off, lied. Over a quarter of a century later Nelson still remained vigorously irate about Cvetic, his contributions to the movie, his testimony at the trials: "HE COULD NOT, NOR DID NOT TESTIFY TO ANYTHING THAT COULD BE CALLED CRIMINAL / ALL HE DID WAS TO SUPPORT THE PROSECUTOR'S READING STUFF FROM BOOKS THE GOV. CLAIMED AS SUBVERSIVE." [30]

Relatively little consensus exists about many of the details of Nelson's life. According to his memoir he was born Stjepan Mesaroš in 1903 in Subocka, a small Croatian village less than fifty kilometers from Bosnia. He recalls arriving in the United States "on a steamy day in mid-July 1920" with his family. An uncle, whom Nelson describes as "a small-time Republican ward heeler," had helped the family come to the country illegally. Nelson's socialism, he remembers, upset the uncle and led him to report "us to the authorities but we were given an opportunity to become naturalized in spite of the violation." The family name in the United States was spelled Mesarosh but according to one obituary he soon adopted the name Nelson, and moved to Pittsburgh in 1923. According to a U.S. Senate committee document ("The Case of Steve Nelson from the Records"), he was born on January 1, 1903 in Chaglich, Croatia, and "entered this country . . . under an illegal and fraudulent passport under the name of Joseph Fleischinger on June 12, 1920." Arrested by immigration authorities two years later, along with his mother and two surviving sisters, their status—asserts the Senate report—was "legalized" in November 1922. [31]

Nelson worked as a carpenter in various U.S. cities with large Slavic communities, among them Detroit. Sometime between 1922 and 1929 Nelson joined the CP. In his memoir Nelson intimates that he joined the CP sometime after being naturalized in 1928. The Senate document argues for the year 1925. In any event, as the historian Theodore Draper notes, Nelson "became a full-time Communist organizer in 1929; was sent to the . . . Lenin School in Moscow in 1931" and "later served as a political commissar in the Abraham Lincoln Battalion during the Spanish Civil War." Nelson recalled the Lenin School as being an academic environment of lectures, readings, and discussion; however, the Senate document repeats the testimony of HUAC witnesses and others who described the school's curriculum as including not only "theoretical studies" but also "military training," "civil warfare, sabotage, secret codes, and conspiratorial organization." The Abraham Lincoln Battalion was part of the International Brigades, made up mostly of Communists, who volunteered to fight for the Spanish government in its struggle for survival against the Nazi-Fascist–backed conservative forces who had rebelled in 1936. After nearly three years of intense bitter warfare the government which had some Soviet support lost. As for Nelson's stint in Spain, which began in 1937, there is no negative mention of him in the literature, except for a defamatory passing reference in one book to a connection between Nelson and the "Soviet secret police." It was active in Spain during the civil war, but whatever one may properly say about the perfidy and malevolent activities of the Soviet secret police in Spain between 1936 and 1939 (between the war's outbreak and conclusion), even Nelson's detractors could not find a convincing way to connect him directly or indirectly with the secret police.[32]

Not too long after the forceful, gregarious Nelson returned from Spain in 1938, the Party assigned him to the West Coast as a "troubleshooter" (his characterization). Because of CP fears about the backlash arising from the August 1939 Hitler-Stalin pact and from the Soviet Union's unprovoked attack on Finland in November 1939, Nelson and his wife in January 1940 "went 'on the shelf' as we called going underground." A few months later Nelson surfaced and became a CP leader in the San Francisco area, where he spent World War II. Some years after the war HUAC among others maintained that Nelson had been involved in atomic espionage. The argument made was that Nelson "instructed . . . a research physicist engaged in the development of the atomic bomb . . . [to] keep Nelson advised of progress . . . in order that Nelson will in turn furnish this information to the proper officials of the Soviet Government." Much heralded by various anti-Communists during the latter 1940s and the 1950s, this charge was never taken to court. But the physicist was tried and convicted of perjury. J. Robert Oppenheimer—who directed the bomb's development—came under suspicion during the war (and subsequently) because of his association in the early 1940s with persons such as Nelson, who was a friend of Oppenheimer's wife (who was the widow of a comrade killed in the Spanish Civil War). Before shrugging off the Senate document's aggressive over-the-top attitude it is worthwhile noting that the FBI had recorded conversations in 1943 in which Nelson "told a Soviet Vice-Counsel about his efforts to recruit scientists at the Manhattan Project," which was building the A-bomb. The evidence that Nelson participated in espionage was probably not untainted enough to obtain a conviction (in large part because much of it, such as the bugging of his home, might not have been admissible). But the evidence is sufficient to suggest that Nelson was no maligned innocent.[33]

Cvetic, despite his later claims, knew little if anything about Nelson's activities on the West Coast; however, after he surfaced, testifying about Nelson's activities in the East became Cvetic's bread and butter. In addition to appearing before congressional committees and giving public lectures and interviews, Cvetic testified in the Smith Act prosecution of Nelson and in the state sedition trials. To keep the attention of Nelson's enemies, Cvetic's statements about Nelson grew wilder and wilder. In 1953, for example, he told a congressional committee that Nelson had declared that getting "suckers in the United States" to aid Communist China would "hasten the revolution in the United States."[34]

In 1952 a Pennsylvania court convicted Nelson of sedition; he was fined $10,000, sentenced to a twenty-year prison term, and ordered to pay court costs of $13,291. Pennsylvania's highest court overturned this verdict in 1954, on the grounds that "the federal Smith Act pre-empted any state prosecution laws where the alleged sedition was against the national government." The state appealed to the U.S. Supreme Court. In 1956 in what has been characterized by the legal history scholar Milton Konvitz as one of "the most controversial cases of the 1955–56 term," the Supreme Court upheld the state court by a vote of 6–3 on the grounds that the Smith Act as a federal law did supersede state law in matters of sedition: the ruling in *Pennsylvania v. Nelson* presented an argument not dissimilar from Hoover's view, who was "against states endangering the work of federal prosecutors, taking away the spotlight from the FBI, and letting loose . . . amateurs to prosecute Reds." As might be expected there was a sharp reaction against the decision. In 1956, forty-two of the forty-eight states (as well as the territories of Alaska and Hawaii) had antisedition or similar statutes in effect, and "in one swoop" the Court invalidated them all. Congressman Howard Smith along with his House and Senate colleagues tried unsuccessfully to get legislation passed that would overrule the Court. In 1958 and 1960 the House of Representatives did pass bills declaring "that only if an act of Congress expressly said that it excluded the states could it be construed as doing so." These bills failed in the Senate, once by only one vote. Nelson, as a Pittsburgh newsman perceptively put it just a few years later, was "destined to be remembered at least by the legal-minded long after the high-ranking American Communists of his era are forgotten." It seemed, however, that Cvetic was not. I could find no comment by him in the mainstream press on the 1956 Supreme Court decision that freed Nelson.[35]

Nor it seemed did he make or at least was asked to make any comment worth recording on another 1956 Supreme Court decision, *Mesarosh v. United States,* which overturned the 1953 Smith Act trial conviction of Nelson and four CP colleagues. This trial, which came only months before the Department of Justice formally decided not to use Cvetic as a witness in any kind of proceeding, marked (as a Pittsburgh newspaper noted) a recognition of sorts: it was "the first time" Cvetic had been summoned by the Department of Justice in a federal court trial as a witness—though he had appeared at other court proceedings. The Court of Appeals for the Third Circuit, because of extensions granted the appellants (including Nelson), did not vote on the case for nearly two years after the initial judgment. In June 1955 the court voted 5–2 to affirm the convictions, but sixteen months later the Supreme Court took a different view.[36]

In October 1956 the Supreme Court ordered a new trial for the defendants, in large part because of doubts about the credibility of one of the prosecution's chief witnesses—not Cvetic, but Joseph Mazzei, whom one commentator labeled "a Munchausen of formidable attainments." Mazzei, whom Cvetic had named as a Communist during his 1950 HUAC appearance, remained an undercover FBI plant until surfacing to testify in the 1953 Smith Act prosecution of Nelson and his codefendants. Mazzei melodramatically revealed that the Party had told him, "to get Cvetic" and to assist in "the liquidation of Senator McCarthy." According to Mazzei, the CP also planned "for the armed invasion of the United States on order of the Soviet Union," and Party officers had taught him "how to blow bridges, poison water in reservoirs, and to eliminate people." Chief Justice Earl Warren speaking for the majority in a 6–3 decision said, "The government of a strong and free nation does not need convictions based upon such witnesses." Referring to Mazzei's allegations about the planned poisoning of reservoirs, Warren stated that such testimony "has poisoned . . . the reservoir and the reservoir cannot be cleaned without draining it of all impurity." Months later, after reexamining the government case "in light of various court decisions," the U.S. Attorney (without mentioning any problems with witnesses) told the press, "We cannot successfully retry these defendants on the basis of evidence presently available."[37]

The system ultimately treated Nelson correctly. But for much of the early 1950s Nelson suffered from what Justice William O. Douglas faulted as a judicial system "often mere mouthpieces of the most intolerant member of the community." Nelson served time, eleven months and twenty-five days in the County Workhouse at Blawknox, Pennsylvania, and in the Iron City jail, and he suffered mentally and physically. But this "political prisoner" (Nelson's view of himself) unlike others such as Arthur Koestler's Old Bolshevik Rubashov suffered no final "darkness."[38]

Musmanno and Cvetic and others abused the judicial system and deserve approbation for much of what they did. But it is important to realize that Nelson was not just a persecuted innocent (e.g., he falsified passport applications; he spent some time in China working for the Communist International). Nelson later called his trials "a shame on America." But he was much more than just "a foot soldier" and a "rank-and-file organizer" (to use the characterizations used by Nelson's collaborators in his memoir); he was, as Theodore Draper succinctly and correctly points out, "obviously a well-known leader just below the top rank, entrusted with one important assignment after another." Yet even that does not excuse the ill treatment meted out to him judicially and physically.[39]

Nelson left the CP in 1957. His son later said that his father quit "while he was a member of the . . . Party's national committee . . . after . . . Khrushchev, the then Soviet leader, denounced the horrors under Stalin's rule." Without any doubt the revelations of that supposedly "secret" speech to the Twentieth Congress of the Soviet CP in February 1956 devastated many of the remaining American Communist faithful. The speech became known in dribs and drabs before becoming public in June 1956. Khrushchev's revelations of Stalin's crimes against his own people and many others were not new to the media in the United States, which as part of America's Cold War propaganda had widely broadcast them in detail. For people like Nelson and those other remaining American Communists their response of shock and anguish rings true and is understandable—as historians John Haynes and Harvey Klehr have pointed out, in the "world of American Communists, Stalin's mass murders were visible only if Moscow could see them. Once Khrushchev gave Moscow's sanctions to the action against Stalinism, American Communists . . . suddenly saw bodies littering the landscape." At the end of a special meeting for Party elite at which Khrushchev's speech was read, Nelson commented, "This was not why I joined the Party."[40]

He and others fought to reform the American CP from within and failed. He and many others left, but not just because of Khrushchev's revelations. To use Irving Howe's words "a dream long corrupted" had been shattered. Nelson recalled some years later that "factors inherent to the movement itself forced me to recognize that the organization to which I'd dedicated my life was no longer a viable means to achieve the kind of social change I envisioned." He found it difficult to make a living once he left the Party. He held a variety of jobs before winding up as a stage carpenter. He retired in 1975. True to his ideals, he was active in the anti-Vietnam war movement and with the Veterans of the Abraham Lincoln Brigade. Nelson remembered that while he was serving as its national commander, Monsignor Rice came to a VALB meeting during the Vietnam war (which both opposed) "and apologized to me." Rice subsequently recalled that later he came to "rather like . . .

him"; it is unclear if that feeling was reciprocated. Nelson died in 1993. Blandon is still on-screen doing bad things but no one now would tie him to Nelson.[41]

I Was a Communist for the FBI bore the usual disclaimer buried in small type at the end of the credits that "the story, all names, characters, and incidents portrayed in this production are fictitious. No identification with actual persons living or dead is intended or should be inferred." But all the publicity, including the trailer, promised the "FACT-FILLED REVELATIONS," the "WHOLE FEARLESS STORY," the "BLAZING AUTOBIOGRAPHY OF AN UNDERCOVER AGENT," the "FIRST STORY OF YOUR FBI'S RELENTLESS COUNTERATTACK!"[42]

The film played up many of the media's exaggerations about Cvetic. He faces ostracism ("Hey, stay away from my kid, he doesn't need your help. Baseball's an American game"). His family is hostile ("You stinking Red! Get out of this house and don't ever come back"). The FBI needs him: it obtains Blandon's plans to cripple Pittsburgh industry, "thanks to Matt Cvetic." His excellent work for the Party earns him an appointment as "chief-organizer . . . for Pittsburgh." Cvetic praises God for being allowed to testify before HUAC and to "crawl out of my rat hole and live like a man again."[43]

The film also added embellishments to Cvetic's story and to the American CP's history that he later incorporated into his version of undercover life. Warner Brothers gave him a "sincere" romantic interest, a schoolteacher who realizes she has been duped and in the approved fashion of the day declares she will name names. Blandon, in gangster fashion, orders her liquidation. An FBI agent sent to protect her is murdered, but Cvetic saves her through a shoot-out with the Communist goons. In a very powerful, well-filmed sequence, Party thugs imported by Blandon use lead pipes wrapped in Yiddish newspapers to beat and silence union officers (including Cvetic's brother) trying to end a wildcat strike called by the CP at a Pittsburgh mill. The newspapers are part of the Communist plan to foment religious strife in the United States, just as the CP is shown inflaming racial tensions. Blandon's speech at a public meeting is designed to foment social violence; at the meeting he refers to African-Americans politely, privately he calls them "niggers." An FBI agent in the film, referring to deaths in the 1943 race riots in Detroit and Harlem, explains "those poor fellows never knew their death warrants had been signed in Moscow." [44]

Years later, the critic Nora Sayre condemned the film as a "sham-documentary." A more perceptive critic, political science professor Michael Rogin, argued that the film "depoliticized the appeals of Communism by using the conventions of the gangster movie and equating Communism with crime." At the time the Warner Brothers production received uneven reviews. Anti-Communism seems to have motivated the more favorable. *The Motion Picture Herald,* an important trade journal whose militantly anti-Communist editor had gushed over Cvetic, judged the film a "major advance in the screen's fight against Communism." The influential Hearst gossip columnist Louella Parsons reviewed the film for the adamantly anti-Red publisher's wire service and called the production "not just another film" but the "strongest exposé of dread Communism to date." The Hearst *Sun-Telegraph* in Pittsburgh also reviewed the film enthusiastically. Surprisingly, the rest of that city's press expressed reservations, although lauding Cvetic. The media centered in New York City responded skeptically to the film, finding it, as one writer observed, "none other than the old gangster . . . formula." Even vociferously anti-Communist *Time* found the film "crude, oversimplified, mechanical." The *Christian Science Monitor* gave the film "a very bad critique." This review, as well as others across the country, expressed concern about the film's inability (in the words of John McCarten) "to have it clear . . . that there's a hell of a difference between liberals and Stalin's little helpers." [45]

Studio executives may have foreseen the more critical reviews, for Warner Brothers had geared up a publicity campaign that anticipated much of the negative response. Warner Brothers did not tout the Cvetic film as one of the studio's "big pictures" of the year but worked hard to sell it. Some months later Jack Warner asserted the effort had paid off, as the film "had chalked up a highly successful box office record." He hedged with regard to exact figures, but whatever the final tally (and one estimate has the film grossing double its production costs), Cvetic certainly benefited from the studio's intensive exploitation campaign. [46]

With this campaign, Warner contributed mightily to the furthering of Cvetic's image as a fearless, self-sacrificing folk hero knowledgeably fighting the Red Menace. To cite just one notable example: *Newsweek's* movie review found *I Was a Communist for the FBI* implausible, but thanks to the studio's efforts, the magazine used stills from the film (with suitably patriotic captions) in a widely distributed pamphlet designed to boost circulation. This pamphlet called attention to *Newsweek's* ongoing uncompromising "exposé of Communism" and equated it to the "authentic story . . . you will see in an exciting . . . timely film" detailing the "risks taken by a single man helping the FBI to rout out Communism." [47]

Cvetic had already hit the lecture trail with some success. But Warner Brothers briefly turned him into a "one-man Chautauqua" (to quote a studio flack) for about a month in an effort to sell the film in the Northeast, although they didn't pay him very well for what they had him do. Just as Cvetic's remuneration for the rights to his story was minimal, so too he earned little touring for Warner Brothers. The studio paid him $500 a week, plus expenses if he stayed overnight outside Pittsburgh—but all too often he wound up back there after midnight. The studio worked him hard. He spoke on the radio, spent time with the local press, addressed community groups. He spoke at luncheons, afternoon teas, dinners, and evening meetings. In Johnstown, Pennsylvania, for example, where he spent less than a day, Cvetic's activities included a broadcast discussion with local law enforcement officials at 11:30 A.M., and less than two hours later a talk and question-and-answer session at a high school assembly. His message did not vary, whether speaking in Johnstown, Albany in New York, or Fairmont in West Virginia: Communists "bore from within" and must be exposed; Americans (especially students) "must be taught" what Communism is. If Americans relaxed their vigilance, Cvetic warned, the Communists would liquidate one-third of all Americans, and for Cvetic, the targeted people always seemed to include those he addressed, whether Lions, Legionnaires, churchgoing students, teachers, or Daughters of the American Revolution. [48]

The Warner Brothers public relations man who shepherded Cvetic on the film promotion tour commented years later that "we built a monster" and remembered unhappily the "starlet-like vanity," lack of polish, pompousness, and "hitting the bottle" (which became such a problem that a two-quarts-a-day limit had to be imposed). Warner Brothers covered up for Cvetic, because it was in the studio's interest to do so, just as it had been for the FBI, which continued to protect him publicly. But Bureau officials sharply reined in Cvetic and Warner Brothers when, in publicizing the movie, Cvetic made statements considered harmful to the FBI's image. Hoover's associates acted quickly, if behind the scenes, to ensure that Cvetic would not repeat what one of them accurately dubbed a "harebrained" charge that the FBI had left in place under surveillance the Communist head of a large California city's water works who "could poison the city's population in a matter of hours." L. B. Nichols, a powerful assistant to the Director and his influential liaison to the media, talked to Warner Brothers and pointed out "they would have to exercise some control over Cvetic" and was assured "it wouldn't happen again." [49]

The Cvetic image also benefited from a radio series, aired initially in 1952, supposedly chronicling his undercover experiences. As with the film, the radio series brought him little money but did keep him in the public eye. The Ziv Company paid Warner Brothers $10,000 for the radio rights to the title "I Was a Communist for the FBI." But Ziv paid Cvetic only $4,000 to "supply his services as an adviser, to waive the right to use his name, and to provide any material he had collected during the . . . years he worked for the FBI." Cvetic also received $1,000 for travel to California (where the show was being set up) and expenses during the three weeks for which Ziv had contracted. The company also agreed during 1952–53 "to set up a paid lecture tour" for Cvetic: $200 plus expenses "per single engagement"; $600 plus expenses for "a week's engagement . . . lectures not to exceed four." In 1958 Cvetic sued the Ziv Company for more than $100,000, charging among other things it had shortchanged him by scheduling as many as twelve lectures a week for which Cvetic received "no additional remuneration." Cvetic, by 1960, had reduced his demands to $10,000. The judge indicated he "would exert every pressure" on Cvetic's lawyer to accept

$2,000; the Ziv Company offered nothing more than a "nuisance value settlement," which would "not exceed $1,000." The lawsuit failed.[50]

That was not the only legal action that resulted from the radio series. Sherman and Moore felt that their contract with Cvetic prior to the *Post* articles entitled them to a percentage of his earnings from Ziv. That company's counsel concurred, asserting that Cvetic "is under certain duties and obligations to them and that, sooner or later, he will have to make his peace with them." Cvetic disagreed, maintaining that the radio series was "a separate venture." They sued. An annoyed Cvetic later reported that his share of "the radio proceeds was only 27 percent, agents and attorneys got the rest." An angry Sherman openly broke with Cvetic. He resented the need to sue, especially as he and Moore never "took a dime" of Cvetic's pay for promoting the film, despite a contractual right to do so. Moore recalls no bitterness on his part. He had "tired of babysitting" Cvetic, whose penchant for women and drink "made him just too much trouble." Martin, the third signatory to the contract, turned the matter over to his agent.[51]

The radio version of *I Was a Communist for the FBI* was produced in Los Angeles. The show had a big budget for its day, reportedly $12,500 per episode. Movie star Dana Andrews played Cvetic in the transcribed series of thirty-minute programs. Jerome Lawrence and Robert Lee, later better known for such Broadway hits as *Inherit the Wind,* scripted many of the episodes. Altogether seventy-eight episodes were produced during 1952 and 1953 (the broadcast cycle then called for thirty-nine original shows with thirteen repeats during the summer). The company, headed by Frederic W. Ziv, an energetic, astute, successful syndicator of radio and television shows, did a splendid job selling the show despite the inroads television had made on radio programming. The company made use of the political climate of the day for commercial ends, garnering sponsors from anti-Communist businessmen and patriotic organizations. The Carter Oil Company, for example, headed by strong anti-Communists, sponsored the program on eight stations scattered across Colorado, Montana, and South Dakota. In various states

American Legion posts obtained local sponsors. All across the country chambers of commerce, unions, and veteran organizations purchased the series for "public service broadcasts."[52]

The radio shows bore even less relationship to reality than the film had. In one episode Cvetic prevents the murder of a liberal editor who realizes the CP has duped him. During the course of another, "The Little Red Schoolhouse," a "comrade from MOSCOW" provokes a college student riot and "a female comrade" masquerading as an American patriot makes love to Cvetic in order to test his loyalty to the Party. The FBI agent who monitored the programs found them "the eeriest kind of cloak and dagger stuff." He judged the writing "poor," the plots "loose," the endings "juvenile." He said, "The one really favorable part of the program is the manner in which the commercials are handled." The historian Richard Gid Powers has noted that Andrews, in his portrayal of Cvetic, "used two voices": as the FBI man the actor "spoke in the earnest All-American tones of radio heroes" like the Lone Ranger; in his Communist persona he spoke with "a sort of boneheaded truculence as though he resented every treasonous moment he had to spend with the comrades." Commenting on this dichotomy and the implausibly tense situations faced each week by Cvetic, a Bureau observer concluded that the radio show "would make any potential informant cringe in terror"–a judgment shared by the annoyed Hoover.[53]

The FBI head, partly because he had anticipated such problems, rebuffed the Ziv Company's overtures. The Ziv people should have guessed Hoover's attitude from the stiff formal limited response to their request about Cvetic's "authenticity." Hoover refused to cooperate in the making or selling of the radio series. In January 1952, when he learned from various field officers that Ziv representatives, attempting to sell the series, had implied Bureau "approval," he demanded that the Ziv sales force stop making "false or misleading statements." An associate of Hoover spelled out the agency's attitude: "The FBI had not endorsed the radio program. . . . [T]he FBI had nothing to do with the promotions of this program, had no comment to make in regard to it, and the FBI was not cooperating in any manner to promote the program." The company speedily agreed to make it clear that the FBI "has not . . . endorsed, approved, or had any connection whatsoever with the radio program." Nonetheless, shortly thereafter Hoover notified all FBI offices that in response to any inquiries the Bureau should "forcibly" and "unmistakably" make it clear that it had nothing to do with the radio program. Notwithstanding the Bureau's attitude, Frederic Ziv, a generation later, still felt positive about shows such as *I Was a Communist for the FBI*. Discussing such programming, Ziv said that in the political context of the 1950s such shows "rendered a proper service."[54]

To sell the series, the Ziv Company sent Cvetic around the country. He gave lectures and appeared on behalf of the sponsors of the show. Local newspapers interviewed him, usually concluding their stories with a mention of the program. Cvetic consistently referred to himself as an "agent" of the FBI, which irritated Hoover. The FBI director, moreover, wanted "no part in Cvetic's promotion." Yet the Bureau seemed unable to rein him in. Cvetic enjoyed the tours, and he certainly benefited from them. The company benefited a great deal more. Depending on the market, the company charged between $13 and $400 for each episode broadcast. During 1952 and 1953, with more than 600 stations signed up each year, that meant a substantial gross income per program.[55]

Ziv did well with Cvetic, but really cleaned up with Philbrick. The company scored a tremendous commercial success with a syndicated TV series based on Philbrick's book. In fall 1953, the TV program *I Led Three Lives*, already one week before it aired, was—according to one study—"scheduled in more markets than carried any of network television's top ten rated shows." Cvetic had been signed first but such popular and financial success as Philbrick would enjoy proved elusive. It has been suggested that Philbrick proved more bankable because Cvetic despite the hype boosting him as a dedicated patriot all too quickly suffered image problems, and therefore Ziv "capitalized on the figure of Philbrick as a . . . narrative anchor around which to build." Once again real financial success had eluded Cvetic. He only grasped how Ziv and Warner Brothers had profited from him later in the 1950s. Then, as he told an FBI agent, Cvetic understood he should have been more concerned with his own situation, he should "have taken better care of Matt."[56]

five

Cvetic's career as a professional witness lasted considerably longer than his brief stay in the limelight. The apogee of that stay came in April 1951, just after Cvetic testified in the IWO case. On April 19 Warner Brothers, with what has been termed "elaborate ceremonies," orchestrated the world premiere of *I Was a Communist for the FBI* in Pittsburgh. Mayor David Lawrence, a shrewd politician who played a major role during the 1950s in a rejuvenation of the city in what came to be called "the Pittsburgh Renaissance," officially proclaimed the nineteenth of April "Matt Cvetic Day." Lawrence presided over a sumptuous "special luncheon" honoring Cvetic at the William Penn Hotel. After lunch came a parade to the Stanley Warner theater, the most important downtown movie house, for the first public showing of the film. That parade went by the courthouse where the first Nelson sedition trial was in progress. Years later a still angry Nelson complained, "The damn thing was playing while my case was going on."[1]

About this time Cvetic began to show signs of that increasing exaggeration that would undermine his credibility and would cause him grief with the FBI, especially its Director. Cvetic basked in his notoriety. HUAC, the *Post* articles, and the movie, as one commentator very aptly put it, had "spoiled Cvetic for the austerity of simple fact." His HUAC testimony contained embellishment here and there, but not much. Soon, however, he moved on to flights of fancy, some of which boomeranged. Hoover, it seems, could live with white lies about the CP and its functionaries; nor does he seem to have been greatly perturbed about Cvetic's testimony on Nelson's statements concerning Communist China seeking U.S. aid, even though as one FBI reviewer put it, "No report submitted by Cvetic can be located which sets out this statement attributed to Steve Nelson." Nor did Hoover exhibit much concern when another Bureau reviewer pointed out that "while the Progressive Party was discussed at many Communist Party meetings in 1948" (information the FBI had gleaned from various sources), Cvetic "exaggerated" when he said "it was discussed at every meeting."[2]

The Director, however, did apparently take umbrage at an invention about a "Nazi spy" and how the "G-men nabbed the Nazi and his radio" after Cvetic took "a look" into the situation. This story, as the Special Agent in Charge (SAC) of the Pittsburgh FBI office put it, had "no basis in fact," and neither as the decade wore on did many of Cvetic's stories. Exaggeration and invention became the staples of Cvetic's lectures and writings. In 1951 the FBI had reined in Cvetic during his promotion of *I Was a Communist for the FBI* when he told one whopper after another. And the Bureau did so again over a year later during the multicity tour Ziv put together for Cvetic to promote the radio series. Without such a governor as the Bureau to rein him in, Cvetic ran loose. Toward the end of the 1950s he was asserting that "the Reds" were "infiltrating the churches in the U.S." and that if the Communists took over "women would be forced into brothels maintained for Red soldiers." But for a short time after he surfaced in 1950 Cvetic had no need to sensationalize, and if he did it was generally inadvertent. He made use of the image created for him to gain lecture assignments about his "undercover" experiences and about his fairly rational prescriptions for dealing with the Red Menace.[3]

Because of Cvetic's notoriety and because of his well-publicized anti-Communist activity Hoover moved glacially in disentangling the FBI from its one-time informant. But act he ultimately did. Hoover had been responsible for "the nonuse" in late 1951 of Cvetic as a witness by U.S. Attorneys in a 1952 Smith Act prosecution in New York City. He tried to achieve the same result with regard to the 1953 Pittsburgh Smith Act prosecution, whose defendants included Steve Nelson. Ever the "compleat" bureaucrat, Hoover moved cautiously at first. In early September 1952 when the question of using Cvetic arose in this prosecution, Hoover ordered that the U.S. Attorneys be made "fully aware" of Cvetic's indiscretions and "questionable statements." Hoover called attention to what he termed "another side of the ledger," but at first without emphasis. He reiterated this warning to the prosecutors a few weeks later because "it is contemplated that Cvetic will be a necessary witness in the Pittsburgh Smith Act prosecutions." These warnings seem to have had some effect, because in February 1953 SAC Pittsburgh called Hoover's office to report he had been told by the U.S. Attorney handling the cases that Cvetic would definitely not be used.[4]

But the Justice Department, apparently unsure about the strength of its case, decided it "essential" that Cvetic testify and informed the Bureau that it would be necessary to use him. A concerned Hoover, once again informed by his associates that "the defense can thoroughly discredit" Cvetic, told them to inform the government attorneys that "the use of Cvetic in any government case would be most unfortunate." The federal government did get the guilty verdict it sought, but Cvetic's credibility came under strong effective attack by the defense as Hoover and his associates had feared, and Cvetic proved a weak reed on the witness stand. Hoover's warnings had correctly stemmed from concerns that Cvetic's problems might not only undermine his credibility but also that of other FBI plants when they surfaced. The straitlaced Hoover, certainly upset by Cvetic's drinking and womanizing, also reacted with consternation to a man developed by the FBI having (as one angry agent said) "capitalized beyond all reason on his position as an informant for the Bureau."[5]

It seems to have taken some time for the Bureau's comments about Cvetic's credibility to make an impact on the other agencies of the federal government that utilized his services. Cvetic was one of the witnesses who testified for the government in proceedings before the Subversive Activities Control Board (SACB), against the Civil Rights Congress in December 1954, and against the Labor Youth League in January 1954. In the latter instance his testimony was deemed "not vital" by a government task force reviewing security witnesses. But it judged Cvetic's testimony against the Civil Rights Congress as "substantial."[6]

The SACB had come into being as a result of the Internal Security Act of 1950, better known as the McCarran Act (after its senatorial sponsor, who inspired, proposed, and strenuously pushed for the legislation). Omnibus in nature, it incorporated a diverse set of antisubversive measures. The legislation, as neatly summed up by one historian, contained "provisions for the registration of Communist-action and Communist-front groups, the emergency detention of persons likely to commit espionage and sabotage, and the tightening of laws against sedition and espionage." President Harry Truman, "who felt it was stupid (the outlaws had to register with the sheriff)," forthrightly vetoed the McCarran Act in a message described by historian Alan Harper as "a masterpiece of its kind"; in essence Truman cogently argued that the legislation "would not hurt the Communists" but "would so greatly weaken our liberties and give aid and comfort to those who would destroy us." The House of Representatives overwhelmingly voted to override the veto. Of the ninety-six senators, fifty-seven voted to override, ten stood with the president, and the remaining twenty-nine turned tail and abstained.[7]

Truman's veto message had asserted that the proposed Board would be "ineffective" and "unworkable," and that "the net result of the registration would probably be an endless chasing of one organization after another." And that proved to be the case. In November 1950 the Board began proceedings to force the CP to register under the provisions of the McCarran Act. Thirteen years later, after much judicial and other travail on the part of the government and the CP, a U.S. Court of Appeals ruled against the government; the decision determined that "the government had found no Party official who could register without thereby laying himself open to prosecution under the Smith Act," which meant no one had to register. The SACB officially passed out of existence in 1973, by which time it had been dead in all but name for over a decade. It never managed to register anything.[8]

However, neither the Civil Rights Congress nor the Labor Youth League long survived the challenge from the SACB, a challenge at least in a small way based on Cvetic's testimony. He testified that the Civil Rights Congress was administered on a day-to-day basis by two Communists and was exclusively preoccupied with defending the pro-Communist Left. The Congress dissolved in 1956 before the Board's 1957 order to register, which thus became meaningless. The Labor Youth League, described as "the youth wing of the Communist Party" by an admirer who overestimated its afterlife influence in arguing that it "loomed especially large" in 1960s campus life, was dissolved by the CP in 1957. While doing so only for a short time, both organizations survived "negative recommendations" from the Justice Department's Committee on Security Witnesses (made up of representatives from the INS and the department's Criminal and Internal Security Divisions). These recommendation were based in part on information supplied by Cvetic.[9]

Not long after his appearance before the SACB, the joint committee, on April 21, 1955, unanimously recommended that "Cvetic not be used as a Government witness unless ... [his testimony] is corroborated from independent sources whether admissible or not." The committee had been in receipt of derogatory information about Cvetic's reliability and veracity from several government agencies, and this precipitated a review of some of the situations where he had testified. The decision had been "not to reopen" with regard to the SACB decisions on the Civil Rights Congress and the Labor Youth League. Cvetic's official usefulness, already clearly compromised, came to an end when, in a deportation case, a June 1, 1955, opinion of the Court of Appeals for the Seventh Circuit characterized Cvetic's testimony as "evasive and conflicting," "hearsay," and of "no more value than the tattlings from a town meeting." The government had erred, according to the opinion, in relying on the credibility of the witness Cvetic.[10]

That credibility had come under strong attack in the deportation and denaturalization proceedings at which Cvetic testified, often as the principal witness. But until that Court of Appeals decision it had not proved possible to counter him effectively. Although denaturalization and deportation proceedings followed different routes, the INS's hoped-for result in all instances was the same: the expulsion from the United States of the party charged. In deporta-

tion proceedings a foreign-born individual had his or her case adju-
dicated at a hearing presided over by an INS official, which in effect
meant that the agency would rule on defending counsel's challenges
to the testimony of a witness it called. Persons who had taken out cit-
izenship papers and had to be denaturalized before becoming eligible to be deported were handled more formally, through
proceedings in District Court rather than at the INS. The numbers
involved were not large. According to one report "335 naturalization
certificates were revoked during the fiscal year ending June 30, 1953;
of these only six were revoked for denial or concealment at the time
of naturalization of membership in the Communist Party." As David
Caute points out, the outbreak of xenophobia during the 1919–20
Red Scare "was more drastic, direct, and brutal": almost 1000 subversives were "deported for political reasons between 1919 and
1921." Only 163 "subversives" were deported between 1945 and
1955. Caute is also correct that obviously the actions undertaken in
the later 1940s and the 1950s intimidated many. The individuals, as
one historian has pointed out, "faced legal consequences mon-
strously out of proportion to any presumed misdeeds they might
have committed.[11]

Cvetic's activity for the INS in this area never gained the
publicity that accompanied his courtroom and congressional committee appearances. But he testified on behalf of the INS in at least
two dozen hearings. No actual record exists apparently. Even
Hoover in retrospect remained uncertain, reporting to his Bureau associates that Cvetic "had been used in approximately twenty such
cases." Certainly the INS worked Cvetic hard. Within a year of surfacing he said about his appearances as a witness for the INS, "I can't
add them up, it is about twelve or fourteen." Cvetic had come to the
attention of the INS during his first appearance before HUAC. And
it was then that Charles Garfinkel, the officer in charge of the Immigration and Naturalization Service in Pittsburgh, had formally requested from that city's FBI permission to use Cvetic as a
government witness. Garfinkel was "desirous of interviewing Matt,
or Matthew Cvetic in connection with several cases pending." SAC
Pittsburgh consulted Hoover about what should be done. The Director felt that previous INS antisubversion activity in places like Dallas

and Seattle had "resulted in considerably [sic] hardship in Bureau's work." But Hoover did not object to SAC Pittsburgh providing Garfinkel with Cvetic's address, especially as it was "public information." The Director also agreed in mid-March 1950 to provide the INS copies of Cvetic's report on a "named subject" (George Pirinsky). But already days earlier a Cvetic associate, newsman Taylor, had reported in the *Pittsburgh Press* that Cvetic had conferred with officials of the U.S. Immigration and Naturalization Service about "Pirinsky alias Zarkoff." [12]

The INS used Cvetic to pinpoint an alien's CP membership or subversive activity (although the definition of such activity remained a matter of contention between the INS and those it challenged). The INS also used Cvetic to testify to a citizen's subversive activity or involvement with the CP prior to naturalization. In the tenor of the early 1950s Cvetic's sometimes extravagant testimony about, for example, CP activity or membership could serve as the basis for INS attempts to deport an individual. Cvetic maintained in his testimony at INS hearings that he served the agency as a "consultant" on a per diem basis. Repeatedly he asserted, "When I function I am paid . . . when I am testifying here as a witness I get paid . . . a day's witness fee." Actually Cvetic had a contract with the INS, which earned him up to $2,400 a year. As an associate reported to Hoover, "Immigration is not anxious to have this publicly known." [13]

The hearings that took place at the INS itself were semijudicial in nature. The individuals under INS scrutiny had counsel, but the proceedings frustrated these attorneys in their attempts to impeach the testimony of witnesses like Cvetic. Schlesinger, for example, tried incessantly to introduce evidence about the darker side of Cvetic's life and to demonstrate that Cvetic's desire for financial gain had a very powerful effect on the content of his testimony in order to cast doubt on his credibility. But invariably Schlesinger and other defense attorneys found themselves stymied by the Special Inquiry Officers overseeing the INS hearings, who would state as did one that he was "satisfied that many adulterers may make credible witnesses" and usually sustained the objections raised by Examining Officers to that line of questioning. Or Schlesinger would prove unable to overcome "objections" to his attempts to demonstrate that Cvetic's "financial gain" served him as "a very powerful motive" in terms of what he testified. At one point an assistant to the extremely agitated Schlesinger sent a memo to the lawyer about his irate responses to Cvetic's testimony: Schlesinger was told that he must understand that the witness's testimony was "calculated to appeal ... mainly to that unfortunate masochistic-sadist and homicidal manic dementia of our population who, I trust, are receiving gentle understanding care in our advanced mental institutions."[14]

Perhaps that is so. But various government agencies reviewed Cvetic's testimony and did not find it lacking corroboration. Cvetic did himself in not so much by what he did on the witness stand as what he did between appearances—and this affected his life, his image, and ultimately the credibility of his testimony. Already in November 1952 Garfinkel "pursuant to telephone instructions" from his superior had spoken to Cvetic about boasting on his speaking tours about lucrative contractual arrangements with the INS (e.g., a $25,000 annual contract). Cvetic admitted boasting about his income to journalists but said that "at no time did he state that this income was in connection with his services" with the INS. Cvetic blamed all misunderstandings on "enemies incurred by reason of his exposing the Communist Party." Garfinkel reported that "I cautioned Mr. Cvetic to refrain in the future from displaying any credentials indicating that he is an employee of our Service and he agreed."[15]

After the 1953 Pittsburgh Smith Act trial a concerned Hoover advised via a series of memos to the Attorney General and to the INS that "derogatory information" available about Cvetic made his use as a witness potentially damaging. The INS, concerned not only about Cvetic but others it had used as witnesses, canceled the consultant contracts of ex-Communists and former FBI confidential informants in July 1954, and in September the Commissioner issued a directive that "deliberately omitted any references to consultants, so that all persons testifying for the INS were to be known as informants or witnesses."[16]

These actions obviously affected Cvetic's income and may have accelerated his drinking. It had always been something of a problem. In 1951 it had increased to such an extent that he joined Alcoholics Anonymous. How seriously he took his participation in AA remains open to conjecture. He described the meetings as "social occasions." In April 1954 he said that it had been "about three or four months" since he had attended an AA meeting, but asserted he had not taken a drink for "about sixteen months, thank God." That may well have been so, but by the end of 1954 he was "off the wagon," had been arrested for drunken driving, and as a result of uncontrollable alcoholism would be institutionalized.[17]

On February 13, 1955, a depressed Matt Cvetic began drinking heavily and apparently nonstop. On February 17, 1955, his son Richard Cvetic had his father admitted to St. Francis Hospital in Pittsburgh, where the admitting doctor after examining the patient recorded that he "was mentally ill from the following facts indicating mental disease: patient is restless, agitated, has a suspicious attitude, seems afraid, admits drinking heavily of late. Is admitted as a chronic alcoholic." Cvetic was not discharged until March 5, after having received four shock treatments. On March 17 Cvetic was readmitted upon "an application" by his son. Cvetic was described by hospital staff as "asocial, withdrawn, depressed, wanders about aimlessly, does not speak until spoken to, admits drinking recently." The hospital discharged him again on March 26. Shortly thereafter, apparently while intoxicated, Cvetic fell, broke his shoulder, spent more than a week in Mercy Hospital, and on being released moved in with his son.[18]

Perhaps not surprisingly, when it learned of Cvetic's problems, the Communist press whooped it up. *The Daily Worker* happily headlined "Reveal Cvetic, Gov't Stoolie Was in Hospital as Alcoholic" and "Cite Electric Shock Treatment for Spy Cvetic's Neurotic Ills." Somewhat more seriously the Western Pennsylvania Committee for Protection of the Foreign Born, a CP front, issued a press release asking for "the immediate reopening of all cases in which Cvetic has testified." Also perhaps not surprisingly, Cvetic's alcoholism did not arouse much compassion in the Bureau's upper echelons either. They understandably disregarded Cvetic's muddled explanations to the Pittsburgh Bureau about receiving "treatment for a 'nervous condition.' " The FBI files released to me that cover this period were heavily censored, but what of Hoover's correspondence was released indicates a concern to protect the Bureau. The Director wrote about Cvetic's foibles to Justice Department VIPs such as the Attorney General (his nominal superior), in which "your attention is called to my letter of . . ." and to the memos sent "for your additional information on numerous occasions." That the exposure shook the Bureau can be gleaned from Hoover's response to the INS Commissioner's request for Cvetic's reports. The Director urged the Bureau to "expedite" and got annoyed when that did not take place. Those FBI staff dealing with the retrieval and transfer of the reports were informed that a memo dealing with the "delay . . . will be placed in the folders of the employees involved." [19]

On March 16, 1955, the head of the INS—presumably after reviewing the delayed files—informed the Attorney General that it "has now ceased using Cvetic." That instruction did not make its way to the Pittsburgh FBI and INS offices until the beginning of April. This hiatus resulted in an interesting coda. John W. McIlvaine, the U.S. Attorney in Pittsburgh, had hoped to use Cvetic "the best known Communist informant in the Pittsburgh area," in a forthcoming series of denaturalization proceedings. Cvetic's problems caused McIlvaine "considerable apprehension," and concern about preparation for cases in which the INS had scheduled Cvetic as the principal witness. Not until April 4 did McIlvaine find that there was "a serious doubt as to Cvetic's credibility as a witness." [20]

Some weeks later at the behest of Hoover, SAC Pittsburgh interviewed Cvetic, who said he felt "all washed up." The FBI agent who spoke with Cvetic assumed from his appearance that he had been "drinking" and found him "extremely depressed." That depression must have deepened when at the beginning of June 1955 the Court of Appeals decision dismissed his testimony. And that depression and the drinking must have contributed to his lackluster, meandering testimony before the Senate Internal Security Subcommittee in mid-June. He inconsistently and almost incoherently spoke about the alleged Communist affiliations of John J. Mullen, head of the United Steelworkers Political Action Committee and a former mayor of Clairton, Pennsylvania. Cvetic accused him of "sponsoring Communist front organizations" among other nefarious deeds. Mullen also testified before the committee, systematically and convincingly; as one observer put it, Mullen "contradicted Cvetic in every particular." Subsequently, "a complete review" by the Bureau of Cvetic's reports found no mention of Mullen.[21]

Why Cvetic performed so badly as a witness is relatively clear. Why he chose to go and testify at all remains open to conjecture. It may have something to do with Mullen's attack on Musmanno, with whom Cvetic remained close. In February 1953 Mullen had charged Musmanno "with trying to have withdrawn a criminal charge"; as mayor of Clairton, Mullen had brought bribery charges against some of that municipality's councilmen. After supposedly being approached by Musmanno, Mullen had gone to the District Attorney who formally accused Musmanno of attempting to hinder prosecution by attempting to intimidate a witness. Ultimately the charges were dismissed and Musmanno was vindicated. However, Musmanno remained irate at what he called "the attempted besmirching" of his name. According to Musmanno's supporters the instigation for Mullen's actions came from the CP and its allies, who wanted to stop the judge's fight against the Communists. A pro-Musmanno press release argued "Mullen's complicity with the Communist Party in Pittsburgh." If the judge had inspired Cvetic to testify, it was a mistake that further destroyed Cvetic's credibility.[22]

Certainly Cvetic generally understood his deteriorating situation. He seems to have comprehended that the Bureau had written him off, if not how thoroughly. And even if Cvetic had not yet been formally notified, he knew that his days as a professional witness for the INS had come to an end. Moreover, Cvetic knew he had not been up to testifying at a Senate hearing. Within hours of that appearance he dropped by the Pittsburgh INS office to tell them that "he believed . . . he may no longer be valuable to the Government as a witness . . . because of the smearing . . . attempt to discredit him because of his drinking and hospitalization." Cvetic told Garfinkel, his INS contact, that he no longer felt able "to stand up to Schlesinger." Cvetic stated that while he would "cooperate with this Service at all times," he did not feel it possible for him to "appear as a witness unless absolutely necessary to the Government."[23]

Before 1955, Cvetic had expressed little concern about his future. Despite the intense criticism he aroused, Cvetic had no reason to do so. He had an interesting life, even becoming a "Kentucky Colonel"—receiving his "commission" in August 1953 at an anti-Communist rally in Louisville at which he spoke on "the workings of the Communist Party in the United States." Apart from the lecture tours organized by Warner Brothers and the Ziv Company, with the attendant publicity these tours engendered, or which the public relations people at Warners' and Ziv could manufacture, Cvetic was sought after because of his supposed expertise. He hired himself out to anyone, official or otherwise, who wished to make use of him. Two appearances bookend that career. Not too long after he surfaced in 1950 Cvetic testified for the defense in the Connecticut court actions resulting from the unsuccessful lawsuit brought by the performers Larry Adler and Paul Draper against those responsible for blacklisting them. Toward the end of 1954 Cvetic testified along with what was characterized as "a parade of . . . informers" in a Kentucky sedition case in which five persons were charged with blowing up a young black couple's house in an all-white neighborhood: the state charged the five, including Carl and Anne Braden, who had deeded the house to the couple, with being part of a Communist plot to "bring about a political revolution" by inciting "racial disturbance and hatred."[24]

As the 1950s rolled on Cvetic served as what columnist Murray Kempton dubbed "a habitual government witness." Cvetic continued to testify before congressional committees, but less and less frequently and with less and less impact on the media. At one hearing he concluded his remarks with the rather pathetic comment to the committee members that "if there is anything I can do at any time, write to me at home." He had passed from being a participant with personal revelations to being a so-called expert, on call as others might require. Indeed, his July 1953 and October 1954 appearances before the Senate Internal Security Subcommittee imply rather strongly that he was now little more than a servant of the rather poorly hidden agendas of others. At both appearances the only senator present was Herman Welker (R-Idaho), who wished to help ensure his Republican senatorial colleague's victory in the 1954 elections against the Democratic candidate—Glen Taylor, a former Democratic senator from Idaho who briefly deserted his party to serve as Henry Wallace's running mate in 1948. During both of Cvetic's appearances Welker zeroed in on the CP "infiltrations" of the Progressive Party, Communist plans for so doing with the Democratic Party, and Taylor. Cvetic did not let down his side: during both appearances he asserted Taylor had been "willing to work with the Communist Party in this coalition" and that Taylor "had made it clear that he was accepting the support of the Communist Party." During the last week of the 1954 campaign the GOP brought Cvetic to Idaho to speak against Taylor.[25]

Cvetic made a comfortable living from his anti-Communism during the first part of the 1950s, but he did not make as much as he boasted or as others thought. At first even the FBI swallowed the tales of "big bucks." In 1950, for example, a close associate of Hoover and someone well versed in public relations wrote with regard to the *Post* series that "word from Pittsburgh now is that [Warners] . . . has bought the story for $75,000." Later, the Pittsburgh papers in reporting on Ziv's investment said it was "believed to be the highest budgeted of all new radio shows," and implied a very good return for Cvetic. The legal contretemps about the sale of the various rights to Cvetic's story made clear how many different ways the proceeds were cut up and how little he cleared. Still, given Cvetic's earning history to that point, he may have initially thought that a rich vein existed to mine. Such did not prove to be the case in the long run. But a 1954 *Nation* article estimated his income "to be as high as $15,000 annually," a not inconsiderable sum, at a time when the median family income in the United States did not exceed $5,000.[26]

Yet overall, Cvetic's anti-Communism did not prove very lucrative. From March 1943 to January 23, 1950, the FBI paid Cvetic a total of $21,967.22, of which the Bureau reckoned $3,474.57 was for expenses. Apart from his limited share of the monies paid for the movie and radio rights to *I Was a Communist for the FBI,* he earned money from the lecture tours set up for him, from speechmaking (as during the 1954 Idaho election where he received as much as $450 for each talk), and from the standard expert witness fee of $25 per day plus $9 daily for expenses (travel was extra and separately reimbursed). The fee was not ungenerous: in Pittsburgh, as a newspaper reported in 1951, the "expert witness fee is the regular $3-a-day plus travel." But it seems that Cvetic did not always understand how to take advantage of a given situation: for his services at the 1951 Pittsburgh sedition trial Cvetic earned only $250 and no expense money; the three other expert witnesses earned respectively (including travel expenses) $1,236, $686, and $360.[27]

Cvetic tried once to capitalize politically on his notoriety. He ran in the May 1954 Republican primary in an effort to become that party's candidate for congressman from the Twenty-Eighth District (central Pittsburgh). A year earlier he had announced his plans to seek the seat held by Herman Eberhaiter, a Democrat. When in April 1954 he plunged in, Cvetic in his campaign emphasized "the nine years that I posed as a Communist for the FBI." For him there was "no compromise with Soviet Russia, her satellites, Red Communism or China." He made much of the fact that Steve Nelson lived in the district, and that it contained the former CP headquarters, a "Communist learning center," and a "Communist Party printing plant"–all this "right in the 28th District." Cvetic told the voters that the legislation he hoped to sponsor would take care of the Communists at home and abroad. For a radio address, his four-page talk had only one short paragraph on "the many other governmental problems which confront all of us every day." His essentially one-note campaign did not impress enough voters to put him on the ticket. He lost the primary to a more established GOP politician but did make a respectable showing.[28]

Cvetic was nothing if not resilient. In May 1955 he gave a talk at a Nevada Air Force Base, "liked the climate," and on July 1, 1955, left Pittsburgh for Las Vegas, where he knew the publicity director of the Sands Hotel. Thanks initially to that man's assistance and to his own skillful exploitation of the Cvetic media image, he managed to eke out a living for a while. He reported to Musmanno some seven weeks after arriving that he was giving talks in Henderson and Reno, as well as surrounding towns. He also wrote the judge: "I'm glad to say the FBI still has faith in me," and that the Bureau had contacted him "in the event . . . [it] might want to discuss any cases."[29]

It did not. The Bureau's only interest in Cvetic was concern over his being "a highly potential source of embarrassment to the FBI." Before leaving Pittsburgh Cvetic had reported to the Bureau there that in Las Vegas he "had an opportunity to work for a newspaper." The Bureau worried that Cvetic might come into contact with Hank Greenspun, editor and publisher of the *Las Vegas Sun* and, as the FBI recognized, "an outspoken critic of Senator McCarthy." From the Bureau's perspective a combination of Greenspun and Cvetic did not bode well. Given its view of Cvetic's "unreliability," the FBI leadership feared that he might "do a Matusow." [30]

In January 1955 Harvey Matusow, well-characterized as one of "the Department of Justice's foremost witnesses," recanted and declared he "had testified falsely in hearings and trials." Matusow's recantation was a powerful bombshell, for he had discredited not just his own testimony, to quote Senator James O. Eastland (D-Mississippi), a veteran anti-Communist lawmaker who headed the Senate subcommittee investigating the "legitimacy" of the recantation, but that of many others. He had been a star witness before various congressional committees, including Eastland's redbaiting Internal Security Subcommittee of the Senate Judiciary Committee. Matusow, who had been applauded for his activity as an "undercover observer" for the FBI, by his recantation cast doubt on the veracity and commitment of such anti-Communist icons as Philbrick and Elizabeth Bentley. As for Cvetic, said Matusow, he "is full of lies purported to be truth. . . . I wouldn't trust him with a 10 foot pole." Matusow's comments were still making waves in July 1955 and would for some time afterward. [31]

The Bureau's fears proved groundless. But concern over how Cvetic might exploit his past ties with the FBI led it to respond to inquiries in a manner that hampered his efforts to find sponsors or financial support. Thus, when a local FBI man queried Bureau headquarters in Washington about how to respond to a third-party inquiry about Cvetic arising from a proposal he had made for a series of talks, Assistant Director Belmont called the agent and advised that while any action was up to him, the potential sponsor "might want to know that Cvetic has made a number of statements during his speeches and appearances . . . which are highly exaggerated and Cvetic's reliability is questionable." The agent so informed the potential sponsor, who although he had been "tempted to go along" with Cvetic, decided "to 'back off' . . . and . . . expressed sincere appreciation for the confidence extended him." [32]

Right after Cvetic came to Las Vegas he spoke with John Cahlan, editor of that city's *Review-Journal*. He hoped for a job at the paper, but that did not pan out. The newspaper did do an extensive feature on him, which contained the usual Cvetic embellishments, including a new one, attempts on his life. Cahlan, although suspicious, was willing through such a feature to make known Cvetic's interest in speaking before civic and social groups in the area. But the editor found "it . . . a little difficult to believe that [Cvetic] . . . can make a living here lecturing and talking." [33]

Cahlan was right. It could not be done. Apart from the FBI's attitude, Cvetic still had a drinking problem—even though he wrote Musmanno about "gaining weight," "swimming," and exercising. Cvetic achieved a reconciliation of sorts with Sherman, who with his family, was driving through on their way back to Pittsburgh. And Cvetic also did manage briefly in December 1955 to latch on to a job as editor of a fledgling Las Vegas weekly (the *Las Vegas Independent*), which in announcing his position played up the *Post* series, the movie, the radio shows, and his "FBI Undercover Activities." However, by February 1956 Cvetic was back in Pittsburgh. He promised various people to straighten himself out and pledged to control his drinking and conduct. [34]

But Cvetic dithered, remained "unemployed" (the Bureau description), and with minimal success gave lectures and talks to groups such as the War Veterans Committee of the Sons of the American Revolution and at functions such as high school commencement exercises (he was "the main speaker" at the Youngwood, Pennsylvania, High School graduation). He also managed to deal with people interested in promoting his past experiences in radio and television and in publishing his book. It may be that his plans to publish a book was the catalyst that transformed FBI's concern about him as a potential source of embarrassment to outright hostility. [35]

Ever since Cvetic surfaced in 1950 he had claimed both publicly and privately to be writing a memoir about his experiences while working for the FBI. At different times the proposed book had various titles, including "I Walked Alone," "Escape to Nowhere," and "They Called Me Comrade." In early March 1955 Cvetic told the Pittsburgh FBI he expected the manuscript to be completed by the end of the month. He reported now having "excellent" help: "a rewrite man" (described by the Bureau as "one John N. Makris . . . of Watertown, Massachusetts") and "two fine grammarians" (identified by Cvetic as Musmanno and William Lynch, a TWA ticket agent at the William Penn). SAC Pittsburgh advised Hoover that "it . . . appears questionable that this office" should review the manuscript since the FBI might later be accused of censorship and Cvetic later might claim his book had the approval of the Bureau. Hoover agreed that it would be undesirable to accept a manuscript of Cvetic's book for reviewing prior to publication, but requested SAC Pittsburgh to advise that "the Bureau would prefer to have the names of the Special Agents named therein deleted."[36]

All this played out against Cvetic's collapse, hospitalization, and shock treatments. L. C. Page, a venerable Boston publisher who had agreed to bring out the book, initially seemed unaware of Cvetic's troubles. L. C. Page's commitment was surprising: he had published "Shirley Temple vehicles" such as *The Little Colonel,* boasted about not publishing "contemporary foreign authors," and was, according to one history, "clearly headed for extinction." Musmanno, who had agreed to do a foreword, did in the words of the publisher, "copious and valuable work" editorially on Cvetic's manuscript. Page seems to have had the completed, revised manuscript in hand by the March 31 deadline. But production was delayed. In a telegram to Musmanno the publisher expressed worry "about possibility of libel in Cvetic manuscript" and said Warner Brothers "are contemplating charging us with infringement of the rights." He also informed Musmanno of "FBI . . . requests." Perhaps the Bureau had persuaded the firm not to go forward. Whatever the reason and despite Musmanno's reassurances, Page canceled publication. "A gentlemanly publisher of the old school" and in his mid-eighties at the time, Page might well have responded favorably to a suggestion from the FBI. Or perhaps he changed his mind for the simpler reason that despite Musmanno's efforts Cvetic's book just wasn't any good.[37]

Whatever Page's reason for not publishing, it was definitely the case that despite the efforts of Musmanno and others, the manuscript Cvetic turned in was beyond rescue in both style and content. Chapter 3, "I'm a Communist for the FBI," begins, "As I became further enmeshed in the Communist imbroglio [*sic*]," and includes such gems as "The heater under the seat in front of mine massaged my feet with soothing heat." Furthermore, this chapter owes more to the movie and reel life, than to Cvetic and real life—which may explain the Warner Brothers response.[38]

Cvetic finally published privately a paperback version of his manuscript in November 1959 under the title *The Big Decision*. The book has little to recommend it. Cvetic learned a few things from his experiences with L. C. Page; he changed all the names of his former CP associates: Steve Nelson became Comrade Beskaroff; Elizabeth Gurley Flynn became Comrade Betti. As for the Bureau: "Names of Special Agents for the Federal Bureau of Investigation have been changed for reasons of national security." Cvetic may have had some professional help, since the book reads much better than the manuscript he turned in to L. C. Page. "The big decision" of the title is Cvetic's acceptance of the FBI's offer "to serve in an undercover role to help thwart the Communist conspiracy," knowing all the disadvantages and sacrifices that would ensue, without any possibility of personal gain. *The Big Decision* does have some basis in fact (e.g., Cvetic's family background, the character of Father Lawless), but much of it hews to the line James Moore earlier had worked out (i.e., Cvetic as unsung self-sacrificing hero, giving his all for the FBI, and thereby losing the respect, love, and admiration of his family and friends, until he surfaces and is received by them with open arms).[39]

Many of Cvetic's undercover and "dangerous" adventures in *The Big Decision* are drawn from the movie and the radio shows. And of course there are old fictions (embellished) such as his encounter with "Captain D . . . , a top Nazi agent, . . . and as ruthless as a cobra." And some new ones such as "the Marxist 'Scientific' techniques of torture and mayhem." Footnoted historical explanations designed to add verisimilitude include "Culture, Recreation, and Entertainment are used by the Reds, solely, for the purpose of promoting the Communist Revolution in the United States." The FBI reviewer of *The Big Decision* dismissed it as "a pocket edition glorifying Cvetic as a Bureau informant in 216 pages . . . , listed to sell for one dollar." He concluded that "this book is a further attempt on his part to capitalize on his former relationship with the Bureau."[40]

After Cvetic surfaced in 1950, those attempts increasingly had preoccupied Hoover and his associates. But until 1956 the Bureau, however it acted behind the scenes, had always dealt gingerly with him. This response changed dramatically in April 1956. Cvetic, frustrated by the failure to get L. C. Page to publish his manuscript, by the necessity in early 1956 to return to Pittsburgh from Las Vegas, and by his lack of immediate prospects, seems to have been negatively vocal about Hoover, the Bureau, and its supposedly better treatment of some other professional witnesses. The FBI reacted speedily and forcefully. On April 6, 1956, SAC Pittsburgh reported to Hoover, that Cvetic "was confronted with statements which he was alleged to have made." Per instructions from Hoover's office, the Pittsburgh FBI did "vigorously interview him." He got a severe dressing down, "straightening him out."[41]

This run-in with the Bureau resulted from Cvetic's jealousy of Philbrick, the middle-level CP official who had surfaced as an FBI informant during the 1949 Smith Act trials. Philbrick had carved out a more successful career as a professional anti-Communist than Cvetic. Philbrick's memoir, *I Led Three Lives* ("citizen, Communist, counterspy"), written with the unacknowledged assistance of the Bureau's public relations arm, became a best-seller and served as the basis for the highly successful Ziv television series. In April 1956, the Bureau learned that Cvetic had charged that Philbrick was "receiving better treatment" and questioned him about statements he had allegedly made accusing Philbrick of having paid "kickback money" to two FBI agents and of being "a left-winger"—charges Cvetic denied having made. Cvetic had also raised questions about Hoover's "drinking." Cvetic was "forcefully told" that he should "shut up," that the "Bureau would not tolerate malicious gossip or false statements regarding the director, the FBI, or Bureau personnel." Cvetic later declared that in 1951, while negotiating with the Ziv Company about the radio series, he had been told that Hoover would endorse Philbrick's story if Ziv used it. Frederic Ziv, on the other hand, recalls that whenever he contacted the FBI about using Philbrick's story, the Bureau would always sidetrack him onto Cvetic.[42]

A contrite Cvetic abjectly apologized but to no avail. As Richard Gid Powers has pointed out, "Once Hoover decided he would not trust someone that person was marked for life." Cvetic continued periodically to send what he described as "a little report" to the FBI, but Bureau policy now decreed that any correspondence from Cvetic not be answered. With rare exceptions that remained Bureau policy until Cvetic's death in 1962. On one occasion, a letter of his did pique Hoover's interest, and agents were sent to interview Cvetic. But in the main his obsequious letters to Hoover invariably went unacknowledged (on them is noted in various hands "no ack. necess."). A Bureau form letter advised groups and businessmen who checked with the FBI that "it in no way" endorsed Cvetic's activities, that he did "not in any way represent the FBI." The Bureau kept a close watch on Cvetic until he died. But when anyone, even a U.S. Senator "friendly" to the Bureau, asked how to contact Cvetic, the FBI simply replied that "no information was available" concerning his "present activities or whereabouts." Cvetic did not seem to have fully grasped the FBI's changed attitude toward him for a long time. He certainly remained unaware of how often the Bureau undercut his efforts to recapture the limelight. A momentary interest by Philbrick's editor in publishing Cvetic's memoirs ended after discussion with a high Bureau official.[43]

The events leading to this betrayal began in Pittsburgh. Toward the end of 1956 Cvetic got in touch with people in different parts of the country requesting financial support for "my personal fight against Communism." Many of those contacted, such as a New York City ad man, did not even respond to Cvetic but just forwarded his letter to the FBI, either in Washington, or locally. In mid-January 1957, Cvetic personally called on an executive of the Westinghouse Air Brake Company in Pittsburgh seeking financial backing, and in support of that plea said he could show him a manuscript dealing with his anti-Communist efforts. The executive advised SAC Pittsburgh that Cvetic was "dropping off his manuscript." SAC Pittsburgh informed the Director that the executive "will do whatever Bureau desires, either review manuscript or make it available." SAC

Pittsburgh wanted guidance, since earlier he had been advised "it would be undesirable to accept manuscript . . . for purpose of reviewing." Hoover instructed SAC Pittsburgh to "immediately obtain . . . manuscript of book, . . . specifically advise . . . not informing Cvetic of action taken." SAC Pittsburgh did as instructed and, after getting the manuscript, made "an autostatic copy"—the original went back to the Westinghouse executive who returned it to Cvetic.[44]

The manuscript SAC Pittsburgh critiqued in detail in six single-spaced typed pages did not differ much from the later *Big Decision*. SAC Pittsburgh concluded that the manuscript generally followed Cvetic's February and March 1950 HUAC testimony. SAC Pittsburgh reported that the manuscript "as a whole implies that due to the FBI's orders as to the secrecy of his work Cvetic was divorced by his wife, separated from his twin boys, disowned by his father, hated by his brothers and sisters, and that he broke his mother's heart." SAC Pittsburgh also found that Cvetic's effort "contains no . . . statements reflecting unfavorably on the Bureau." SAC Pittsburgh concluded his detailed review by reporting that on January 25, 1957, the Westinghouse executive had telephoned the Pittsburgh Bureau to inform the FBI that Cvetic had just told him that Herbert Philbrick was reading the manuscript and that Doubleday had offered a "substantial advance." Cvetic also happily told this to an FBI agent whom he accidentally met in downtown Pittsburgh. Cvetic said he had sold his manuscript to Doubleday, had written it "in plain language," had eliminated all "preachments," and needed to make only a few revisions. The Westinghouse executive had told SAC Pittsburgh that he did not know if Cvetic's claims were "true or not." They were—but would not be for long.[45]

On February 6, 1957, the Doubleday editor called L. B. Nichols and reported that Cvetic's manuscript had made a favorable impression. This editor, who while at McGraw-Hill had been responsible for the publication of *I Led Three Lives,* said he had discussed the manuscript with Philbrick. The editor also stated that all references in Cvetic's manuscript to the FBI "were very commendatory and favorable," wondered if the Bureau would like to read the manuscript, and asked "if there was anything he should know about the author." On an off-the-record basis Nichols told the editor that "we have been disappointed" in Cvetic's "subsequent develop-ment," that he was "a far cry from Philbrick," and was "lacking in character." Nichols further told the editor that he should know that an exposé had appeared on Cvetic in the *Daily Worker* on being hos-pitalized for excessive drinking. Nichols added that he had told the editor all this "only on a personal and confidential basis as he always had been decent to us."[46]

On February 18 Nichols reported that the editor, on Febru-ary 13, had decided not to publish Cvetic's book. In the interim Dou-bleday had stalled Cvetic, "haggling" (to use his word) with him over details in the manuscript. He felt they were "quibbling" but believed the company would place his book in line for publishing on their fall-winter calendar. On February 13 Cvetic reported to SAC Pitts-burgh that Doubleday "at the very last moment . . . walked out on our proposed agreement." He did not have any inkling of the FBI's role in this decision. Cvetic believed that the impetus for the change of mind came from those who had dogged him all along: "Some self-serving, 'well-intended' person gave them some real 'inside' infor-mation." Nichols, before speaking with the editor, had advised the Director and his close associate Clyde Tolson that "if I can get the hooks into it I intend to do so," and he had.[47]

The Bureau discouraged interest of any kind in Cvetic. When Gerald Govorchin, a professor of history at the University of Florida putting together a history of Americans from Yugoslavia, wrote the Bureau in an attempt to get a photo of Matt Cvetic for the book, he was fobbed off in a letter signed by Hoover: "I would like to be of assistance . . . we do not have a photograph . . . available nor do we have his present mailing address." However, the professor proved resourceful, got in touch with Cvetic, and obtained from him a photo. Unfortunately Govorchin relied on the *Post* series and infor-mation from Cvetic for the section "Spy for the FBI."[48]

Cvetic did not realize the FBI was doing him in. But on a visit to its Pittsburgh office in February 1957 he told the agents that while "he has no regrets about anything that he did in the past . . . he does regret that he did not take better care of 'Matt.' " It was a senti-ment he echoed during a lengthy May 1957 *Pittsburgh Press* interview in his "small . . . hotel room": Cvetic told the interviewer that too late he learned that "the fellows who were slapping me on the back, telling me what a great guy I was, had their hand in my pocket." Cvetic not only recounted what he had done over the years but added some of the usual exaggerations, such as the Nazi agent, plus some new ones such as fending off with "my .38 which I am forced to carry" a former comrade who came "after me with a butcher knife."[49]

The interview was an obvious pitch for support in his avowed "fight against Communism." And over the coming months he hustled to achieve media visibility and financial backing. He wrote an open letter to President Eisenhower, released to a press that was uncaring and indifferent, even in Pittsburgh. He sent out what the FBI characterized as a "tract" as well as letters to the editor to "leading news agencies in the country," all to no avail. He got in touch with former supporters such as the American Legion indicating he "would be most happy to offer . . . my personal knowledge"; the Legion ignored his letter. As in the past Cvetic wrote to prominent people in Pittsburgh and elsewhere but got only perfunctory replies. The Bureau reported that Cvetic, having received "routine" responses from Vice-President Nixon "had shown" the letters around as a sign of official support.[50]

It was not merely the FBI's antagonism that caused Cvetic's almost total failure to elicit interest in his proposals (although the Bureau's influence certainly should not be discounted). Times had begun to change; anti-Communism no longer could attract the attention it had just a bit earlier. Cvetic's drinking and instability had become public knowledge; indeed, he alluded to them in detail in the *Press* interview. His protestations of having learned his lesson and given up drinking might have had the desired effect, if he had not simply used up his credibility. At the end of January 1958 he resettled in Los Angeles, accepting as he later put it "the advice of the 'fellas' who counseled me to go out to the West Coast to get a fresh start." He flew there without being "too definite in his own mind" about what he expected to be doing.[51]

Before he left, SAC Pittsburgh advised him that in line with Bureau policy the FBI expected that Cvetic "in conjunction with any public appearances . . . must be factual and truthful and must not build up or embellish." Cvetic indicated that he understood this. Toward the end of February 1958, about a month after leaving Pittsburgh, he had made up an advertising brochure announcing his availability for speaking dates. It referred to the *Post* series, the movie, and the radio show, and advertised "Nine Years a Communist for the FBI." Cvetic did manage to interest a *Los Angeles Times* ad man, who wrote letters of support for him, got stories into the *Times,* and contacted acquaintances such as the then influential columnist Walter Winchell. Nothing succeeded.[52]

Despite the lean pickings Cvetic seems to have enjoyed Los Angeles. He had "an exchange of correspondence with Groucho Marx," was "photographed for the . . . media" while attending a seventy-first birthday party for the actor William Frawley (then one of the stars of the fabulously successful TV show *I Love Lucy*), and claimed to be in negotiation "with several producers" over his book, reporting "we will be in production here before not too long." To avoid seeming a one-man operation, he revived his Robert Stanton pseudonym, signing it as "Administrative Assistant" in various mailings.[53]

But as Cvetic admitted to some of his correspondents, for a while it was "touch and go." Yet ultimately he found his métier, the towns and smaller cities of America west of the Mississippi. He played on his media image and on his former FBI ties. He was not too proud to umpire a Pony League baseball game in South Dakota. And he kept his fees reasonable for the venues to which his self-promotion brought him: for towns with a population of 5,000 or less he charged $150, for communities with populations between 5,000 and 25,000 he charged $200, and for places whose population ranged from 25,000 to 50,000 he charged $250. His fees "included all expenses." He spoke in places ranging from Casper, Wyoming, to the South Dakota Black Hills. There, he reported, "we wowed them." A St. Paul civil servant in early 1959 found Cvetic "not a very dynamic speaker" but felt "his meeting was a huge success."[54]

Cvetic rescued himself from this difficult existence by attaching himself to "the Radical Right," a political movement which flashed into prominence, especially in southern California, during the early 1960s. Cvetic became closely involved with the John Birch

Society, described in an Anti-Defamation League report as "the spearhead of the Radical Right." He also established ties with the "Fright Peddlers," especially the Christian Crusade, the personal anti-Communist fiefdom of the Reverend Billy James Hargis, characterized by that same report as "one of the more flamboyant evangelists of the Radical Right." Cvetic, as during his days as a professional witness, never really escaped from the ranks but he was a dutiful foot soldier who benefited from his association with these groups. And, of course, his promises to the Bureau notwithstanding, he continued to play up his one-time FBI ties. All his promotional literature for *The Big Decision* and for his speechifying, even his calling cards, contained the words "former FBI counterspy."[55]

His newfound affiliations benefited him in various ways. The Radical Right made great use of paperbacks to sell its ideas and pump them into mainstream public opinion; one 1960s report found that sales of books pushed by this movement "compare favorably with those of popular books on the national best seller lists." Cvetic's *Big Decision* benefited—the effectiveness of the Radical Right in this area seems to validate Cvetic's claims in March 1961 that "we were on the 50,000th copy" (well, perhaps it was a bit less) and in November 1961 that the book would be going into "a 4th printing and going stronger than ever." At $1 a copy, however, the profit must have been minimal. John Rousselot (R-California), identified as "one of two known Birch members" in the House of Representatives, placed Cvetic's October 1961 *Christian Crusade* article "Communists in Agriculture" in the *Congressional Record,* stating Cvetic "knows what he is talking about."[56]

Thanks to his newly won ties Cvetic secured more prestigious speaking arrangements. He spoke at the August 1960 Christian Crusade Convention in Tulsa, damning Communists and praising Hoover as "one of the greatest Americans today." Cvetic's speech in San Diego at a luncheon meeting of the Association of the U.S. Army represented another breakthrough, especially given the attendant publicity and media reportage. Nearly three hundred persons attended, according to one press account. A description of the meeting forwarded to Hoover commented favorably on Cvetic's presentation and said he "had thought up some sharp answers."[57]

An ability to deal with the language, not always present in his earlier endeavors, now marked his efforts. An article by him in *The American Mercury* (a once great literary magazine that had become a vehicle for all kinds of extremism including "blatant anti-Semitism") cleverly followed the extremist line in dealing with what Cvetic dubbed "The Mental Health Goldbrick." Cvetic also got other right-wing media exposure as he attacked "pseudo-intellectuals" and "self-styled liberals" opposed to the John Birch Society, discussed "Communists infiltrating our churches," and exposed the comedian Steve Allen, the industrialist Cyrus Eaton, Mrs. Eleanor Roosevelt, and Dr. Linus Pauling—each as "a promoter of Communism." Cvetic peddled by mail, and wherever he spoke, reprinted excerpts of his testimony before the Senate Internal Security Subcommittee.[58]

An attempt by the Bureau to deal with Cvetic's publicity makes clear why those opposed to the Radical Right described southern California at that moment as a place where "one finds the voice of the cuckoo shrilling loudest in the land." A lengthy Cvetic "letter to the editor" of the *Los Angeles Times,* prominently displayed, used the words "Ex-FBI Agent" in the heading. Close associates of Hoover who knew his policy on Cvetic told SAC Los Angeles "to contact a good friend on the paper and informally advise him" about Cvetic. SAC Los Angeles did as ordered and reported back that he had been informed that Cvetic had not received special treatment: "The man in charge of their 'Letter to the Editor Section' was so anti-Communist that he would prominently display any anti-Communist letter."[59]

Cvetic seems to have pulled himself together and gotten his drinking and anxieties under control. He had a young woman associate described as "beautiful," and in 1961 it was reported that they would soon wed. He worked hard for the John Birch Society as a recruiter and as a speaker for the Christian Crusade. On July 26, 1962, Cvetic died of a heart attack while waiting to take a driver's exam at the Hollywood branch of the California Department of Motor Vehicles. Obituaries on both coasts spent space on the *Post* series, the movie, and the radio shows, and the myths they had propagated outlived him. Those who had used Cvetic to further their anti-

Communist agenda had been more successful with the Cvetic story than they had realized. The *Los Angeles Herald-Examiner* reported how his mother died "believing her son a traitor." The *New York Times* described Cvetic as "a former counterspy for the Federal Bureau of Investigation." His funeral took place in Pittsburgh: it was according to one account "not a hero's good-bye, just family, and a few friends."[60]

Controversy dogged Cvetic for much of his public life, and continued to do so even for a while after his death. *Newsweek*'s obituary described him as "a self-proclaimed former undercover agent" for the
FBI, which maintained, according to the magazine, that his only
connection with the Bureau "was as a paid informer." This death notice brought the FBI inquiries from around the country. The
Bureau's response, however it was framed, whatever the words written for the Director to sign, always included in some form the
phrases "Matthew Cvetic was not a Special Agent. . . . He assisted
the Bureau by furnishing information from February 1943 to January
1950."[1]

After Cvetic died, as his brother Ben reported, "some people said there was foul play involved" in his death. A fund-raising
brochure for a foundation designed to memorialize him and to dis-
tribute *The Big Decision* carefully stated that on the day he died, "Matt
had a sandwich at a . . . coffee bar" and though there were "lingering
rumors Matt had been fatally poisoned in that lunch room, killed by
a Communist . . . an autopsy would not confirm this." True enough,
the coroner's report stated that he found "absolutely no evidence of
foul play. . . . Cvetic suffered from a significant arterial sclerosis
which was sufficient to cause death by heart attack." But some true
believers remained dissatisfied, at least for a time.[2]

The paranoia that caused this brief flap over the end of
Cvetic's life typified the cast of mind that marked many of the Radi-

cal Right's most committed supporters. That movement suffered the normal fate of extremist movements in America. As the historian Arthur Schlesinger Sr. pointed out at the time, "Each upon reaching its peak speedily declined, as if the public, surprised at itself, suddenly recovered its balance." Cvetic's death spared him another failure, of the kind that the proposed foundation suffered, and as did the Christian Crusade and the John Birch Society. An ultimate lack of public support marginalized these momentarily powerful groups into ineffectualness.[3]

Cvetic's career is a cautionary tale. He seems to have been more an opportunist than a committed anti-Communist in any serious, ideological sense. He was just a kind of low-grade guy, doing a job, without any special animus against those on whom he informed or against whom he testified (not even Nelson). His motivations do not seem to stretch beyond trying to aggrandize himself. He did not act out of spite or maliciousness, the effects of his occasionally fanciful testimony not withstanding. He tried to ride the crest of the anti-Red wave in the early 1950s, succeeded for a while, then, because of his personal shortcomings, fell into obscurity.

Unreliability was one of Cvetic's great failings. Who can take seriously his 1954 testimony to a Senate committee about "a Communist conspiracy planning to liquidate a large percentage of our population, and planning to put many of us into forced labor"? And the flights of fancy became ever more absurd as the years wore on. Nevertheless, his 1950 HUAC testimony avoided excessive exaggerations and had a solid grounding in fact. One may not like the talebearer for being a "snitch" but in Cvetic's case he initially provided a wide array of information about the CP and its tactics in the Pittsburgh area and elsewhere. He did "out" many hitherto unknown Communists; he did deal intelligently with the Party's infiltration and manipulation of front groups and CP cadre; he did touch on episodes of espionage which archival revelations have at least partially substantiated. His 1950 testimony unquestionably smacked of self-promotion, and the media's use of Cvetic's revelations inflicted distress on dozens of people. "Still," as historian Ellen Schrecker asserts in a somewhat different context dealing with such testimony, "it was clear that something was going on."[4]

Attention must be paid to the targets of his charges and to the source of the charges directed against him. In the Cvetic story there are no heroes. I am certain that both FBI Director J. Edgar Hoover and Pittsburgh attorney Hyman Schlesinger would resent being grouped together—yet there does not seem to be all that much difference between a Hoover who accepted Cvetic as an FBI plant, and a Schlesinger who relentlessly and ruthlessly attacked Cvetic for all his foibles but never would admit to any of his own. Indeed, Hoover and Schlesinger, although on opposite sides of the political fence, knew how to operate in ways well beyond Cvetic's abilities. One need not go as far as did the screenwriter Dalton Trumbo, who two decades after being blacklisted declared, "It will do no good to search for villains or heroes or saints or devils because there were none; there were only victims." It seems to me that a bit more is at stake. Even a scholar unfriendly to Cvetic and his ilk asserts that "the Communist reality was sufficiently impressive to give some validity to the fears of its enemies." And ultimately a 1999 history of the Cold War sums up the situation: "A prevailing paranoia did not mean there was nothing to be paranoid about."[5]

Cvetic had surfaced as a fighter against the Red Menace in Pittsburgh and was an integral part of the anti-Communist drive in that area during the early 1950s. Indeed, his activities outside Pittsburgh notwithstanding, Cvetic's anti-Communist career at its height publicly centered on combating and exposing any kind of subversion assumed active in that city and the surrounding area in western Pennsylvania.

That Cvetic both there and nationally got brief but intense favorable public exposure speaks volumes about the temper of the times in which he flourished, and underscores why he and his career deserve attention. Monsignor Charles Owen Rice, a responsible, dynamic, and sometimes overly vigorous Pittsburgh anti-Communist leader during the early heyday of the Cold War who knew Cvetic reasonably well, has characterized him as a "schnook" and a "schmuck," who needed handling. Rice also knew Cvetic's non-FBI handlers reasonably well and believes the political temper of the time allowed them to make him a public figure with impact. Ultimately "a certain native shrewdness" allowed Cvetic to escape them (recalls Rice, "I think Matt jumped before he was pushed. He wanted to get out there and make some money . . ."). But he did not manage to operate well on his own.[6]

Cvetic obviously benefited enormously from the heating up of the Cold War in the late 1940s. That conflict has been usefully described as "the most remarkable *polarization* of politics in modern history." And this assessment is one with which most scholars of the period agree (whatever their point of view on the causes of the Cold War). The icy moment marking the exact outbreak of that conflict remains a matter of bitter debate among scholars and many others. Yet whatever dispute and ambiguity surround that moment, whatever the myriad often contradictory controversies concerning the Cold War's onset, there can be no doubt that by the late 1940s the United States was fully engaged. The administration of President Harry Truman was waging that war firmly abroad and at home.[7]

The Truman administration's campaign needed villains: American culture has always demanded the existence of villains. At many moments in modern U.S. history the proponents of "the" American way of life, in order to justify it, need enemies—real or imagined, domestic and/or foreign. Cvetic benefited from that needed enmity, and from the fact that, for most mid-century Americans, the Left well filled that role. As historian Peter Buckingham points out, although "the word 'Left' refers to a wide variety of positions . . . all . . . these political labels have been misused . . . through the years." Popular culture damned "the Reds." Politically even "pink" became for many a pejorative label. With rare exceptions *all* shades of Red have come under vigorous, often unreasonable attack—as alien, as threatening, as "un-American." Thus, in one "Red scare" after another, the serious, significant political and practical differences among Communists, Socialists, and any other brand of Marxism have been ignored, and they have been lumped together as "the Red enemy."[8]

Within the United States in the later 1940s fear of the Soviets and their supposed domestic agents, whether justified or not, resulted not only in a Red scare but often near-panic. The writer Willie Morris found it "understandably difficult for the young American of the 1990s to comprehend the horrendous fears of international

Communism in the Fifties, the inexorable Red tide moving aggressively across the globe . . . , finally toward, for all one knew, Kansas City." Cvetic and his handlers took advantage of this situation. It may well be, as historian John Haynes has incisively argued, that it is a myth that for over a decade "most Americans were so obsessed with domestic Communism that hysteria ruled the land." Yet for a significant number of Americans at least some of the 1950s proved terrifying. The militant anti-Communists reflected, especially in a heavily ethnic Pennsylvania, what has been cogently described as "the deeply held views of a large section of the public, including the lower and middle classes." [9]

During the Korean War, whose duration (1950–53) coincides with the high tide of Cvetic's notoriety, and in the months immediately before and after, the Establishment media waged a vigorous campaign to mobilize public opinion against Communist subversion. The flames of domestic anti-Communism were fanned in order to garner support for the government's anti-Soviet stance abroad. These years have been aptly described by historian Guenter Lewy as "an age of suspicion," during which "a national fetish with anti-Communism pervaded American society." Although this fetish never totally captured American public opinion, historians have argued with justification that this Red scare weakened civil liberties and impugned traditional standards of tolerance and fair play. The writer David Caute has argued in hyperbolic fashion that a "great fear" settled over the United States and has maintained perhaps too forcefully that Cvetic contributed significantly to "Hell in Pittsburgh." Scholars of varied political stripes have argued that for *some* years open dissent in the United States nearly disappeared as "rampant" Red-baiting "narrowed the range of . . . utterances and ideas" and the "anti-Communism of the majority was translated into near unanimity." But even at the height of their power Cvetic and his ilk everywhere in the United States did not manage to totally stifle dissent or opposition. [10]

A culture in such a tense condition needs heroes, maybe even more than villains. Some American heroes, even the noble George Washington, temporarily dip in public esteem, but ultimately remain firmly ensconced in the American pantheon. However, most of those applauded as heroes in their heyday, such as Cvetic, soon face eclipse. They enjoy only a brief burst of glory: like Washington's fellow generals—for all their contemporary approbation—they fall into the dustbin of history drawing attention only from the most diligent of scholars. During the height of the Cold War both Red-baiters and others eulogized individuals such as Elizabeth Bentley, Louis Budenz, Angela Calomiris, Bella Dodd, Hede Massing, and Boris Morros—to name only a few of the defectors and undercover agents who have left behind autobiographical accounts. At one time these individuals commanded much more attention than did Cvetic (indeed, for a variety of reasons he could not find a commercial publisher for his memoir). The media generally hailed them enthusiastically for combating the Red Menace as well as for the self-sacrifice imputed to them for such activity. However, they soon faded from view, the fate of their books a telling clue about their rush to obscurity. Columnist Joseph Alsop's 1951 comments on the Bentley memoir serve as a telling critique on it and similar books: he wrote how "very hard" it was "to decide" whether to treat her effort "as tragic, or as ludicrous, or as terrifying, or as pathetic."[11]

Even Whittaker Chambers ultimately did not fare all that well. He garnered what seemed lasting celebrity for his charges against Alger Hiss, accusing him of being a spy and a Communist: Chambers's autobiographical effort achieved much critical praise, but not enough to overcome what the critic Lionel Trilling described as the "loathing" of those who rallied to Hiss. President Ronald Reagan in 1984, twenty-three years after Chambers's death, awarded him a posthumous Medal of Freedom, the nation's highest civilian honor. Yet over the years Chambers has receded from the consciousness of all but the most interested partisans of both men. Once upon a time the Hiss case, and consequently Chambers, had been an agonizing cause célèbre. Yet already by the end of the 1950s Chambers, to use an admiring biographer's words, had been displaced: "the instrument of history . . . had become its relic"—notwithstanding a first-rate monograph on the case that appeared a generation after its genesis and persuasively argued Hiss was "guilty as charged." Only in the mid-1990s, with the death of Hiss (which evoked much comment) as well as the publication of a masterful biography of the long-dead Chambers, did the latter once more briefly enter into the limelight.[12]

Some Cold War anti-Communists, neither as important nor as talented as the multifaceted if flawed Chambers, remained longer in the public spotlight, among them Herbert A. Philbrick. The first FBI plant to surface, he wrote (apparently with the help of the Bureau) a best-selling book about his experiences as "Comrade Herb" while working for the FBI.[13]

Subsequently, the Ziv Company—a pioneering, successful TV syndicator—transformed *I Led Three Lives* into an extremely profitable, influential, long-running TV series. Ziv produced 117 half-hour episodes of what is commonly understood to be one of "the earliest Cold War forays into mass culture." The show ran weekly between May 1953 and mid-1956; reruns ran well into the 1960s. As Cvetic well understood, such media exposure can be very useful: the series not only boosted Philbrick's career as an anti-Communist lecturer and writer, but also allowed Richard Carlson—the actor portraying Philbrick—to lecture profitably about the show, the Cold War, and "subversion."[14]

The Communist Party was not just another brand of social democracy. Communists did put themselves unstintingly and heroically on the line for a wide variety of admirable causes (e.g., civil rights). But thanks to the secrets unearthed from archives, East and West, it has become clear that a significant number of Party members were used for causes that had little to do with their social concerns and, in the words of one history, worked for the Soviet Union as "agents, mail drops, and couriers." Some of those who make the loudest cries about the "prevailing paranoia" in the United States during the height of the Cold War express little concern, for instance, about Communist activity of a less socially correct kind. A 1997 review of the "Washington witch hunt" of government employees in the decade after World War II claims passionately, and with conviction, but with relatively little direct evidence, that more than twelve thousand men and women "after being investigated, reinvestigated, and further reinvestigated, decided to quit their jobs" and that "more than 2,700 Federal workers [were] ordered to resign or else."[15] But apart from failing to provide a reliable source for such statistics (and one must consider that hundreds of people leave government service every day for every possible reason), this polemic resolutely refuses to recognize that there might be another side to the equation among the tens of thousands of federal employees. The Soviet Union did make use of some Party faithful in ways inimical to the United States. One must unhappily take into account (to use the words of a leading U.S. counterintelligence operative) "that there were U.S. citizens . . . willing to betray this country." [16]

Events in the world at large also had an enormous impact. The revelations in early 1946 about the Soviets using Communist sympathizers in Canada to spy on that country's activities, the creation in 1946–47 of Soviet satellite states in Eastern Europe, the February 1948 Communist coup in Czechoslovakia, and the Berlin Blockade of 1948–49 heightened the already prevailing worry in the United States about radicals, especially Communists. Whatever the reasons for these secret actions, they concerned many Americans and helped to make Cvetic–who attacked Communists at home and abroad–a not unattractive figure.

There is no question that Cvetic damaged people's lives. But who were these people, and even more important why could a Cvetic do them harm? A significant number, unfortunately, were hapless individuals who suffered for their political beliefs, as was often the case with the INS attempts to denaturalize and deport persons who could not be of any harm to anyone or anything. But much of the answer to these questions lies in the very essence of the American Communist movement–not so much in its programs as its operations. Cvetic could do the damage he did because of a very mistaken policy on the part of the CPUSA. The Communists at the forefront of various social actions often did not reveal themselves as Party members, even in favorable environments. Communist Party secrecy had a corrosive effect, as those being manipulated (even in very noble causes) became aware of it. Ellen Schrecker, certainly an outspoken foe of McCarthyism, is unfortunately right on target when she insists that the "CP's attempts at secrecy . . . were self-defeating. They fooled no one and just reinforced the Party's image as a conspiracy," as a sinister movement that needed to be exposed by people like Cvetic. [17]

Cvetic's testimony was of two kinds: he named names, and he spoke about what "they" had done. His inability to do the latter without exaggerating led properly to his discrediting. The FBI, whatever the reason, publicly at least displayed relative restraint in its antisubversive activities. Cvetic, once he surfaced and formally cut loose from the Bureau, fell into the hands of those in government and in other arenas such as journalism who were wildly eager to exploit the Red Menace. Unfortunately, Cvetic—a man of little personal substance—took his cues from them. He tried too hard to please when he had no need to do so. He did not, for example, have to put words in Nelson's mouth. Nelson was an avowed Communist with a track record as part of a tough CPUSA cadre. Cvetic should have stuck to the facts. As it was, government agencies knew more about Nelson and his activities than Cvetic ever could or would.

In terms of naming names Cvetic surprisingly proved more circumspect. Not until his last days as a professional witness when desperate not to be cast aside, did he go beyond the pale, as with his charges against Mullen. But Americans do not like a "stoolie," even one like Cvetic, presented as a self-sacrificing patriot. And once the myth wore thin, Cvetic, who had antagonized its creators, proved unable to sustain his image. On the whole, for better for worse, Cvetic was correct in his claim that "no one successfully challenged my sworn testimony" when it dealt with Party membership. In other aspects he proved much less reliable; embellishing did him in.[18]

In Pittsburgh the response to Cvetic and other professional witnesses cost several hundred people their jobs. As UE archivist David Rosenberg has pointed out, "While we had no Gulags here and no state-sponsored psychiatric wards for dissenters, we had . . . torment and destruction of health and livelihood visited on individuals." The media, in playing up Cvetic (and others), significantly contributed to the problems faced by Pittsburgh's Communists and fellow travelers. Years later a journalist there felt that "things might have been blown out of proportion," but added, "It wasn't yellow journalism. We felt that we had to report . . . news." There were horror stories such as Nelson's unwarranted incarceration, but in the main the courts (despite leftist lawyer Victor Rabinowitz's assertion that they "were of no help whatsoever") did serve as a bulwark against the excesses of the Pittsburgh media, sustaining him against Cvetic not once but twice. Nelson never did receive a bullet in the nape of his neck; twice the courts sustained him against Cvetic.[19]

In 1953, about the time that Nelson went to prison, John Oakes—a *New York Times* editorial writer and a member of the family that owned that newspaper—wrote a friend, "It is my thought that while the United States is in no sense in a 'wave of terror' and where there is no genuine hysteria regarding spies and Communists," McCarthyism has had "a profound effect." But within a relatively short time that effect had worn off. What had been front-page copy in the Pittsburgh newspapers in 1950 had no impact in 1955. Already in 1954 the Pittsburgh newspapers reported that, despite a Cvetic charge before a Senate committee about a man's "alleged Communist affiliations," city officials deferred action pending study—and the *Post-Gazette* gave more than equal space to the man's denials. By the end of 1956 the newspaper would treat sympathetically a postal clerk discharged as a "subversive," cleared, and finally reinstated, not identifying him and referring throughout all the stories to "Mr. X."[20]

Some two decades after Cvetic died, many of those he named still referred to him as "evil" and as a "bastard"—a reporter found "animosities as fresh as ever." But Schlesinger's widow in 1980 expressed no bitterness: she said, "We never regretted getting started with Communism. It was worthwhile. When you're involved . . . it keeps you busy and alive. I'm an old woman now and bored with life." Joseph Rudiak, a former head of the American Slav Congress in western Pennsylvania and in 1980 a fifty-year veteran of the Party, which he joined at age nineteen, opined that "Cvetic made things tough" but said he no longer harbored any hard feelings toward him; he believed that "people took advantage of Matt . . . he went through hell."[21]

There is no need to feel sorry for Cvetic. He was not an admirable man. He lived a deceitful, generally unattractive life, marred by alcoholism, womanizing, and emotional instability. He betrayed his friends and supporters both before and after he surfaced as an FBI informant. Because of petty greed, stupid recklessness, and an indifferent morality, he damaged himself, his family, and a host of other people. Just before his death he wrote one of his sons, "There is not one in Pittsburgh who can do me any good. . . . There are a few bastards who would like to hurt me."[22]

All these flaws notwithstanding, it seems to me that ultimately Cvetic was a sad figure, and that his life is a sad tale–not because he proved unable to capitalize on his FBI experiences, not because the media exploited him, and not because the FBI turned on him. The sadness lies in the fact that someone like Cvetic had the impact he did, that the standards of American society had become so twisted that a Cvetic becomes a hero. Steve Nelson was not beyond reproach. But he was absolutely right in asserting that the saddest part of Cvetic's story is that he "was believed."[23]

That Cvetic, unlike so many other professional anti-Communists, is still remembered at all has nothing to do with his place in history. He is not unique. There were many other active anti-Communists, many of whom played more important and dramatic roles in the domestic Cold War. They, like Cvetic, had a symbiotic relationship with the media. Yet it has been a long time since they fought Red subversion in print, on screen, and over the national radio and TV airwaves. But Cvetic battles on as a Communist for the FBI wherever and whenever a TV station broadcasts the film *I Was a Communist for the FBI*.

The Nazi propagandist Dr. Paul Joseph Goebbels, a great movie fan as well as a successful ladies' man, once asserted that "in propaganda, as in love, anything is permissible." And so it was with Cvetic. A myth was built up. The myth existed before the movie. Hollywood habits pushed the Cvetic story into familiar genre, and the myth became cast in concrete. The Cvetic story as set forth on screen was not particularly successful as a movie in its day but as the continuing underpinnings for a myth it defies challenge.[24]

The movie even has an afterlife on the Internet–almost all references to Cvetic on the web are to the movie. All else about him seems forgotten. No matter how bad the film was, no matter how far from reality, *I Was a Communist for the FBI* continues to shape images of the Cold War, the Communists, and Matt Cvetic. Those media images underscore political filmmaker Costa-Gavras's words about how for film it is "easy to manipulate," to transform "the false idea into a good," to present "a completely different version of what society was really like." For us the Cold War has ended, the evil empire has broken up. But *I Was a Communist for the FBI* remains history and reality.[25]

And as such it remains a vivid reminder of how Matt Cvetic was sold to the American public as an anti-Communist icon. The Cold War took place a long time ago, but there are still lessons to be learned from it, especially about how the media manipulates reality. Those types who created, nurtured, and exploited Cvetic are still with us. His story though far in the past still has lessons for us now.

Notes

Introduction

1. Hartley, quoted in John Gardiner, "Lost Victorians," *History Today,* December 1999, p. 18; Jacob Weisberg, "Cold War Without End," *New York Times Magazine,* November 28, 1999, p. 121. Philip Jenkins, *The Cold War at Home: The Red Scare in Pennsylvania, 1945–60* (Chapel Hill: University of North Carolina Press, 1999), because it deals with events in Cvetic's home state—as might be expected—devotes some space to him (pp. 4, 21, 30–33, 35, 40, 66, 75–84, 100, 112–13, 115–16, 121, 153–54, 158, 162, 167–68, 181, 188, and 192), albeit much of the mention just blandly quotes his charges and implies exaggeration and falsification on his part. Cvetic gets very limited play in Richard Gid Powers's comprehensive *Not Without Honor: The History of American Anti-Communism* (New York: The Free Press, 1995); Powers devotes only one paragraph (p. 252) to Cvetic, and most of it deals with the fanciful movie made about his activities. A sampling of other 1990s works does not offer much on Cvetic. Griffin Farriello, *Red Scare: Memories of the American Inquisition–An Oral History* (New York: W. W. Norton, 1995), pp. 98, 208–9; M. J. Heale, *McCarthy's Americans: Red Scare Politics in State and Nation, 1935–1965* (Athens: University of Georgia Press, 1998), p. 208; Ellen Schrecker, *Many Are the Crimes: McCarthyism in America* (Boston: Little, Brown, 1998), pp. 127, 138, 151, 229, 392.

2. K. G. Robertson, ed., "Introduction," in *War, Resistance, and Intelligence: Essays in Honour of M.R.D. Root* (Bernsley, South Yorkshire: Leo Cooper, 1999), p. xvii.

3. Jenkins, *The Cold War at Home,* p. 75.

4. On the title page of his self-published memoir, Cvetic is described as a "former FBI counterspy" (Matt Cvetic, *The Big Decision* [Hollywood, Calif., 1959]). The Bureau consistently in response to inquiries about Cvetic stated that he "was not a Special Agent of the FBI" (see, for example, in the months after Cvetic's death, John Edgar Hoover to [name deleted], Safford, Ariz., December 26, 1962; Hoover to [name deleted], Jacksonville, Fla., February 6, 1963; and Hoover to [name deleted], Hot Springs, Ark., May 3, 1963–all in FBI file no. 100–372409 "Matthew Cvetic" [hereafter "FBI Cvetic"]). This distinction may seem minor, but to Hoover, who believed that agents had a special cachet, that differentiation was very important.

5. Richard H. Rovere, "The Kept Witnesses," *Harper's,* May 1955, p. 34.

6. Matt Cvetic, as told to Pete Martin, "I Posed as a Communist for the

FBI," *Saturday Evening Post,* pt. 1, July 15, 1950, pp. 17–19, 92–96; pt. 2, July 22, 1950, pp. 34–35, 52–55; pt. 3, July 29, 1950, pp. 29–30, 100–102; Jonathan Mumby, *Public Enemies / Public Heroes: Screening the Gangster from "Little Caesar" to "Touch of Evil"* (Chicago and London: University of Chicago Press, 1999), p. 213.

7. [Name deleted,] Pilkino Anti-Graft Movement, Inc., Manila, The Philippines, to the FBI, June 20, 1992, FBI Cvetic, is typical of such inquiries.

8. Hoover to Special Agent in Charge (SAC) Pittsburgh, May 6, 1955, FBI Cvetic.

9. M.R.D. Foot, quoted in Mark Seaman, "Good Thrillers, But Bad History," in Robertson, ed., *War, Resistance, and Intelligence,* p. 28.

Chapter 1

1. Rudolph M. Susel, "Slovenes," in Stephan Thernstrom, ed., *Harvard Encyclopedia of American Ethnic Groups* (Cambridge: The Belknap Press of Harvard University Press, 1980), p. 935; Gerald Gilbert Govorchin, *Americans from Yugoslavia* (Gainesville: University of Florida Press, 1961), p. 76.

2. As with so many aspects of his life Cvetic's recollections prove contradictory. In his 1959 memoir he recalls that "both Mom and Dad had told me stories of . . . how, in 1890, they had come to America" (Cvetic, *The Big Decision,* p. 16). But when he surfaced in 1950, he said that his parents had come to the United States "fifty years ago" (Cvetic as told to Martin, "I Posed as a Communist," pt. 1, p. 92). Louis Adamic, *My America* (New York: Harper & Brothers, 1938), pp. xiii, 164; Roger Daniels, *Not Like Us: Immigrants and Minorities in America, 1890–1924* (Chicago: Ivan R. Dee, 1997); *Saturday Evening Post* editor George Horace Latimer, quoted in Adamic, p. 191; John A. Fitch, *The Steel Workers,* with a new introduction by Roy Lubove (1910; Pittsburgh: University of Pittsburgh Press, 1989), p. 10. Matt Cvetic as told to Pete Martin, "I Wore a Red Mask for the FBI: Rough Draft–Long Version–Before Checking with Lawyers," pp. 84–85 (hereafter cited as "Cvetic, 'Red Mask' "), in *I Was a Communist for the F.B.I.,* Warner Brothers Archives, University of Southern California (hereafter cited as "WB USC")–this draft reproduced the contents of thirteen Dictaphone belts containing the conversations and interviews *Saturday Evening Post* editor Pete Martin had with Cvetic, which served as the basis for the three-part "as-told-to" series in that magazine. Because they had no idea about what had served as a basis for the *Post* articles, the lawyers who later intensively cross-examined Cvetic in a variety of cases and hearings and caught him in a series of contradictions, which he managed to shrug off as Martin's literary license, never called Martin to the witness stand. Also, Cvetic as told to Martin, "I Posed as a Communist," pt. 1, p. 94; SAC (Special Agent in Charge) Pittsburgh to Hoover, February 26, 1942, FBI Cvetic.

3. Cvetic, *The Big Decision,* pp. 16, 158; "Cross Examination of Matthew Cvetic by Hyman Schlesinger, August 10, 1954," *In the Case of Hyman Schlesinger,* UE/Labor Archives, University of Pittsburgh, Pittsburgh, Pa. (hereafter cited as "UE Archives"); J. R. Thornton, SAC Pittsburgh to Hoover, February 26, 1942, and SAC Pittsburgh to Director FBI, November 11, 1947, both in FBI Cvetic; U.S. Congress, House Committee on Un-American Activities (HUAC), *Hearings,* "Exposé of the Communist Party of Western Pennsylvania, Based Upon the Testimony of Matthew Cvetic," 81st Congress, 2d sess., February 21, 1950, p. 1196 (hereafter cited as "HUAC Cvetic" by date and page); "Cvetic, Matthew C." (Background Information in Em-

39. SAC Pittsburgh to D. M. Ladd, January 2, 26, 1949; SAC Pittsburgh to Hoover, August 22, 1949, both in FBI Cvetic; Cvetic as told to Martin, "I Posed as a Communist," pt. 3, p. 100.

40. Cvetic to Martin, "I Posed as a Communist," pt. 3, p. 100; Hoover to SAC Pittsburgh, November 1, 1949, FBI Cvetic.

41. Hoover to SAC Pittsburgh, May 7, 1948, and SAC Pittsburgh to Hoover, March 8, 1948, both in FBI Cvetic.

42. SAC Pittsburgh to Hoover, December 23, 1948; SAC Pittsburgh to D. M. Ladd, January 4, 26, 1949; and Hoover to Tolson, no date (probably early January 1949)–all in FBI Cvetic.

43. Nicholas N. Kittrie and Eldon D. Wedlock, Jr., *The Tree of Liberty: A Documentary History of Rebellion and Political Crime in America* (Baltimore: Johns Hopkins University Press, 1986), p. 356.

44. Hoover to SACs, New York City and Pittsburgh, January 26, 1949; SAC New York City to Hoover, February 15, 1949; Hoover to SAC Pittsburgh, June 8, 1949; and SAC New York City to Hoover, no date (probably late May, early June 1949)–all in FBI Cvetic.

45. Cvetic as told to Martin, "I Posed as a Communist," pt. 3, p. 100; Cvetic, "Red Mask," pp. 18, 80; Cvetic to [name deleted], FBI Pittsburgh, to SAC Pittsburgh, and to Director FBI, September 23, 1949, and SAC Pittsburgh to Hoover, August 22, 1949–all in FBI Cvetic.

46. Hoover to SAC Pittsburgh, September 1, 1949; F. J. Baumgardner (Internal Security Section Chief) to SAC Pittsburgh, November 22, 1949; SAC Pittsburgh to Hoover, December 9, 1949; and F. J. Baumgardner to SAC Pittsburgh, December 20, 1949–all in FBI Cvetic.

47. Hoover annotation on p. 5 of F. J. Baumgardner to H. B. Fletcher, subsequently Assistant Director, October 5, 1949; SAC Pittsburgh to D. M. Ladd, December 28, 1949; and SAC Pittsburgh to Hoover, January 4, 1950–all in FBI Cvetic.

48. Daniel J. Leab, "Anti-Communism, the FBI, and Matt Cvetic: The Ups and Downs of a Professional Informer," *Pennsylvania Magazine of History and Biography* 115 (1991): 535–81; interview with Monsignor Rice, August 16, 1988; telephone interview with Steve Nelson, September 19, 1989; Arthur J. Sabin, *Red Scare in Court: New York versus the International Workers Order* (Philadelphia: University of Pennsylvania Press, 1993), pp. 176, 190; Sabin to Leab, March 23, 1992 (letter in author's possession); *Pittsburgh Post-Gazette*, February 20, 1950, Newspaper Carnegie Pittsburgh.

49. "Investigation Procedures," *In the Case of Hyman Schlesinger*, UE Archives.

50. IWO Trial Record, pp. 2446, 2510, 2616, 2346.

51. SAC Pittsburgh to Director FBI, June 25, 1950.

52. J. H. Plumb, quoted in Robin Winks, *Cloak and Gown: Scholars in the Secret War, 1939–1961* (New York: Quill/Morrow, 1987), p. 499, n. 30; Caute, *The Great Fear*, p. 216.

Chapter 2

1. *Pittsburgh Sun-Telegraph*, quoted in Curtis D. Macdougall, *Gideon's Army* (New York: Marzani & Munsell, 1965), p. 218; Karl M. Schmidt, *Henry A. Wallace: Quixotic Crusade of 1948* (Syracuse: Syracuse University Press, 1960), p. 133.

2. Richard J. Walton, *Henry Wallace, Harry Truman, and the Cold War* (New York: Viking Press, 1976), p. 272; Schmidt, *Henry A. Wallace*, p. 133.

3. Arthur Miller, *Timebends: A Life* (New York: Grove Press, 1987), p. 341.

4. Ronald Gregor Suny, *The Soviet Experiment: Russia, the USSR, and the Successor States* (New York: Oxford University Press, 1998), p. 326; Ronald E. Powaski, *The Cold War: The United States and the Soviet Union, 1917–1991* (New York: Oxford University Press, 1998), p. 62. See also M. K. Dziewankoroski, *Poland in the Twentieth Century* (New York: Columbia University Press, 1977), pp. 118–59.

5. Alistair Cooke, *A Generation on Trial: U.S.A. vs. Alger Hiss* (New York: Knopf, 1950), p. 340; Norman Moss, *Klaus Fuchs: The Man Who Stole the Atomic Bomb* (London: Grafton Books, 1987), chap. 8. A fascinating and unusual overview to Fuchs's actions is a collection of materials (especially the interviews) for a West German documentary, "Klaus Fuchs–Atomspion," in a March 1990 special issue of *Celluloid.*

6. Richard Fried, *Nightmare in Red: The McCarthy Era in Perspective* (New York: Oxford University Press, 1990), p. 120.

7. "The Mystery of the Kidnapped Russian," *Life,* August 23, 1948, pp. 23, 25, 27.

8. HUAC, *Hearings Regarding Communist Infiltration of Radiation Laboratory and Atomic Bomb Project at the University of California, Berkeley, California,* 81st Congress, 1st sess., April 22 and 26; May 25; June 10 and 14; August 14; and September 14 and 27, 1949. There had been executive sessions regarding the subject in 1948, but only a few pages had been made public months later. The hearings continued in the 1950s: see *Hearings Regarding Communist Infiltration,* 81st Congress, 2d sess., December 20, 21, and 22, 1950, and *Hearings Regarding Steve Nelson (Including Foreword),* June 8, 1949, 81st Congress, 1st sess., p. viii. Senate Judiciary Committee, Subcommittee to Investigate the Administration of the Internal Security Act, *Hearings on Proposed Antisubversion Legislation,* appendix to part 1, "The Case of Steve Nelson from the Records," 88th Congress, 2d sess. (hereafter cited as "Senate Judiciary Committee, 'Steve Nelson' "), summarizes all the information available from public records to the compiler(s) on Nelson, who is described as "a very typical Communist and professional revolutionist." Cvetic's testimony (much of which had by then been laid open to question) serves as substantiation for various charges in this appendix.

9. Merlyn Pitzele, "Can Labor Defeat the Communists?" *Atlantic Monthly,* March 1947, cover, p. 28; Steve Rosswurm, "Introduction: An Overview and Preliminary Assessment of the CIO's Expelled Unions," in Rosswurm, ed., *The CIO's Left-Led Unions* (New Brunswick, N.J.: Rutgers University Press, 1992), p. 11.

10. James Matles and James Higgins, *Them and Us: Struggles of a Rank-and-File Union* (Englewood Cliffs, N.J.: Prentice Hall, 1974), p. 138; Dan Tracy, president of the AFL's competing International Brotherhood of Electrical Workers, in 1940, quoted in Galenson, *CIO Challenge to the AFL,* p. 255; resolution quoted in David Shannon, *The Decline of American Communism* (New York: Harcourt, Brace, 1959), p. 216.

11. McCarthy's Wheeling speech supposedly referred to 205 subversives in the State Department, and that is what newsmen there reported. During the course of the senator's speaking tour that number fluctuated. The text of his Wheeling speech, which he later placed in the Congressional Record gave fifty-seven as the number of subversives (Senator Joseph McCarthy, "Speech at Wheeling, West Virginia, February 9, 1950," in Ellen Schrecker, ed., *The Age of McCarthyism: A Brief History with Documents* [Boston: Bedford Books of St. Martin's Press, 1994], pp. 211–16). Richard

Rovere, *Senator Joe McCarthy,* with a foreword by Arthur M. Schlesinger, Jr. (1959; Berkeley and Los Angeles: University of California Press, 1996), pp. 132, xii.

12. Edwin R. Bayley, *Joe McCarthy and the Press* (Madison: University of Wisconsin Press, 1981), p. 217.

13. James Wechsler, "The Journalism That Failed," *The New Leader,* December 14, 1981, p. 5.

14. Telephone interviews with James Moore, August 12 and September 26, 1988.

15. Ibid.

16. *Pittsburgh Post-Gazette,* December 15, 1942; Kermit McFarland, "Traveling Judge," *Pittsburgh Press,* November 14, 1943; "Biographical Data–Blair F. Gunther," "Gunther Sketch–For Use Anytime," and "Information from the Campaign Committee," in Newspaper Carnegie Pittsburgh.

17. Gunther obituaries in *The New York Times,* December 24, 1966; *Pittsburgh Press,* December 23, 1966; and *Pittsburgh Post-Gazette,* December 23, 1966; Special Agent [name deleted] to [name deleted], June 1944, in SAC Pittsburgh to Director FBI, February 21, 1951, p. 6, FBI File no. 105–13439 "Americans Battling Communism" (hereafter cited as "FBI ABC").

18. *Pittsburgh Post-Gazette,* December 15, 1942; "Biographical Data–Blair Gunther," Newspaper Carnegie Pittsburgh.

19. Kermit McFarland, "When It Comes to Commies, Gunther Is a 'Gumshoe,' " *Pittsburgh Press,* March 19, 1950.

20. HUAC, "Report on the American Slav Congress and Associated Organizations," April 26, 1950, summarized in *Digest of the Public Record of Communism in the United States* (New York City: The Fund for the Republic, 1955), p. 628; Senate Judiciary Committee, Subcommittee to Investigate the Administration of the Internal Security Act, *Hearings on Communist Propaganda,* pt. 2, 83d Congress, 2d sess., October 7, 1954, p. 61; *Pittsburgh Press,* April 26, 1942. The criterion for an individual being screened was "membership in, affiliation with, or sympathetic association with" designated organizations; that was a determining factor "as to whether the employment or retention in employment in the Federal service . . . is clearly consistent with the interest of national security" (*Digest of the Public Record of Communism,* p. 68; see also pp. 68–75 for a listing and court decisions with regard to a listing to 1955).

21. Margaret Collingwood Nowak, *Two Who Were There: A Biography of Stanley Nowak* (Detroit: Wayne State University Press, 1989), p. 185; Special Agent [name deleted] to [name deleted], June 1944, in SAC Pittsburgh to Director FBI, February 21, 1951, p. 6, FBI ABC. A much more positive assessment of the American Slav Congress than that set forth by HUAC is to be found in an article by Mary Cygan in Paul Buhle, Mari Jo Buhle, and Dan Georgakas, eds., *Encyclopedia of the American Left* (New York: Garland Publishing, 1990), pp. 28–29.

22. *Glas Ludowy* (People's Voice), a Polish newspaper published in Detroit, April 39 [*sic*], 1949, p. 1, quoted in SAC Pittsburgh to Director FBI, February 21, 1951, p. 13, FBI ABC; Bagehot quoted in Colin Ingham, ed., *Man and Affairs: A Modern Miscellany* (Sydney: Currenwong Publishing, 1967), p. 22; McFarland, "When It Comes to Commies," *Daily Worker,* April 12, 1946, quoted in Director FBI to the Attorney General, September 23, 1950, p. 3, FBI File no. 62–93021, "Blair F. Gunther" (hereafter cited as "FBI Gunther").

23. SAC Pittsburgh to Director FBI, September 22, 1950, p. 1, and Director FBI to the Attorney General, September 23, 1950, p. 1, both in FBI Gunther.

24. A prothonotary is a chief clerk in some U.S. state courts. *Pittsburgh Press,* September 15, 1964.

25. Obituary, *Pittsburgh Press,* July 23, 1987 (This clipping comes from the *Press* morgue; it is now in the hands of the *Post-Gazette,* which took over that daily and which makes those files available to researchers—hereafter cited as *"Press* morgue"); Rice to Leab, October 7, 1988, p. 2, and February 25, 1955; W. A. Branigan, Washington, D.C., to A. H. Belmont, September 15, 1953, FBI File no. PG 62–1787, "Harry Alan Sherman" (hereafter cited as "FBI Sherman").

26. Obituary, *Pittsburgh Press,* July 23, 1987, *Press* morgue.

27. Obituary, *Pittsburgh Post-Gazette,* July 23, 1987; James J. Smith, III, "Harry Alan Sherman, Esq.," *Pittsburgh Legal Journal* (1987): 40; *Pittsburgh Press,* January 4, 1956, clipping, FBI Sherman; SA [name deleted] to SAC Pittsburgh, June 2, 1950, FBI File no. HGG2–80892, FBI Sherman.

28. *Pittsburgh Press,* December 5, 1943, August 30, 1944, February 6, 1945, and June 22, 1950, *Press* morgue.

29. David Oshinsky, "Labor's Cold War: The CIO and the Communists," in Robert Griffith and Athan Theoharis, eds., *The Specter: Original Essays on the Cold War and the Origins of McCarthyism* (New York: New Viewfronts, 1974), p. 124.

30. Harold K. Birney to Federal Bureau of Investigation, May 11, 1943, FBI Sherman; *Pittsburgh Press,* December 5, 1944, December 6, 1944, *Press* morgue; minutes of the Executive Board District Council, July 23, 1944, "Struggle for Control of Local 615," no date, p. 80, FBI Sherman (part of a larger report; the Bureau seems to have had an excellent pipeline into both the local and national boards, since it had access to all minutes); *Pittsburgh Press,* November 5–6, 1944, *Press* morgue; "The Industrial Union Advisor," February 15, 1945, in Cvetic file, Musmanno Papers; *New York Times,* November 5, 1944, clipping, FBI Sherman.

31. "Harry Allan [*sic*] Sherman versus the UE," undated, pp. 7, 9, FBI Sherman (this in-house review seems to have been completed toward the latter part of 1945, since it does not go beyond that date, and covers in sometimes confusing and occasionally inaccurate detail Sherman's relations with the UE); *Pittsburgh Press,* January 25, 1945, *Press* morgue; excerpts from Judge Harry Rowland's opinion (concurred in by both other judges on the panel), *Pittsburgh Press,* March 29, 1945, *Press* morgue.

32. Senate Judiciary Committee, Subcommittee to Investigate the Administration of the Internal Security Act, *Hearings on Subversive Influence of the United Electrical, Radio, and Machine Workers of America,* 83d Congress, 1st sess., November 9, 1953, pp. 24, 25.

33. Ibid., November 10, 1953, p. 119.

34. *Pittsburgh Sun-Telegraph,* July 23, 1953; "Jewish Culture Verboten," pamphlet, *In the Case of Hyman Schlesinger,* UE Archives.

35. "Letter to Director, Re: Yiddish Kultur Farband, Inc.," January 26, 1955, p. 1; *Pittsburgh Post-Gazette,* June 11, 1955, FBI File PG 62–1787, FBI Sherman.

36. *Glas Ludowy* (People's Voice), November 26, 1949, quoted in SAC Pittsburgh to Director FBI, February 21, 1951, p. 17, FBI ABC.

37. Jenkins, *The Cold War at Home,* p. 75; "Attorney Harry Allen [*sic*] Sherman, chairman of Americans Battling Communism, will address members of the B'nai Emunch Men's Club . . . on 'Communists in our Midst,' " *Pittsburgh Press,* November 22, 1950, *Press* morgue, and "Harry Alan Sherman, chairman of the Americans Battling Communism, spoke at Bethel High School last night," *Pittsburgh Press,*

June 22, 1951, *Press* morgue. *Pittsburgh Press,* October 3, 1947, and *Pittsburgh Post-Gazette,* October 23, 1947, both in FBI ABC. On February 21, 1951, the Pittsburgh FBI sent a report to Hoover "regarding the organization American Battling Communists, Inc." Most of the information in the report came from Pittsburgh newspapers. SAC Pittsburgh to Director FBI, February 21, 1951, FBI ABC. Ronald Schatz, *The Electrical Workers,* p. 202.

    38. *Pittsburgh Sun-Telegraph,* October 4, 1947; *Pittsburgh Press,* October 4, 1947; and *Pittsburgh Press,* October 23, 1947—all in FBI ABC.

    39. *Pittsburgh Post-Gazette,* November 6, 1947, FBI ABC; *Pittsburgh Press,* October 31, 1947, *Press* morgue.

    40. ABC charter quoted in *Pittsburgh Press,* November 23, 1947; Director FBI to SAC Philadelphia, November 16, 1950, FBI ABC.

Chapter 3

    1. J. Edgar Hoover, "FBI Reveals How Many Reds Live in Your State," *Look,* August 1, 1950, p. 69.

    2. O'Reilly, *Hoover and the Un-Americans,* p. 230; Daniel J. Leab, ed., *Communist Activity in the Entertainment Industry: FBI Surveillance Files on Hollywood, 1942–1958* (Bethesda, Md.: University Publication of America, 1991), microfilm.

    3. "Addendum," February 17, 1950, attached to H. B. Fletcher to Mr. Ladd, February 16, 1950, FBI Cvetic.

    4. Hoover's notes on *Washington Times-Herald,* February 23, 1950, and *Washington Post,* February 24, 1950, clippings, FBI Cvetic.

    5. Director FBI to SAC Pittsburgh, May 8, 1950; SAC Pittsburgh to Director FBI, July 5, 1950; L. P. Nichols to Mr. Tolson, July 19, 1950; and Hoover to [name deleted], Boston, Mass., August 16, 1950—all in FBI Cvetic.

    6. IWO Trial Record, pp. 2674–75; telephone interviews with James Moore, August 12 and September 26, 1988.

    7. Interview with Sherman [by name deleted], report to Hyman Schlesinger, p. 1, *In the Case of Hyman Schlesinger,* UE Archives; Sherman to Hoover, October 9, 1953, "Memo to Mr. Boardman," no date, no. PG62–1787, FBI Cvetic. Sherman was not a modest man. At the time of Cvetic's initial HUAC appearances he told the committee "I am Matt Cvetic's attorney. . . . I am also attorney for Americans Battling Communism, the organization to which Matt originally came for advice as to how to make his knowledge public, and in my capacity as attorney for Americans Battling Communism as well as his personal attorney, as I became . . . , I reviewed the data he was going to use as the basis of his testimony. . . . I might say it took many hours of reading and going through a lot of other papers to reduce it to what finally came . . . into Cvetic's possession for the purpose of testifying. . . . Matt . . . was instructed by me, and followed my advice very closely" (HUAC Cvetic, February 1950, p. 2370).

    8. *Pittsburgh Press,* February 19, 1950; *Pittsburgh Sun-Telegraph,* February 19, 1950.

    9. F. J. Baumgardner to A. H. Belmont, April 3, 1950, script attached, pp. 1, 2, 4, FBI Cvetic.

    10. Ibid., script, pp. 7, 8.

    11. *Pittsburgh Press,* February 20, 21, 1950; *Pittsburgh Post-Gazette,* February 20, 21, 1950.

12. February 21, 22, 23; March 13, 14, 24, 25; June 22; September 28; and October 13 and 21.

13. Frank Donner, *The Un-Americans* (New York: Ballantine Books, 1961), p. 142; *Pittsburgh Post-Gazette,* March 1, 1950; *Pittsburgh Press,* March 1, 13, 1950 (another Taylor story); Winks, *Cloak and Gown,* p. 406.

14. SAC Pittsburgh to Director FBI, March 13, 1950; Letter to Director from Pittsburgh, June 21, 1950; and D. M. Ladd (Assistant Director) to the Director, March 17, 1950–all in FBI Cvetic.

15. D. M. Ladd to the Director, March 17, 1950, FBI Cvetic; HUAC Cvetic, March 1950, p. 1352.

16. IWO Trial Record, p. 2674; HUAC Cvetic, February 1950, pp. 1201, 1245.

17. IWO Trial Record, p. 2648; HUAC Cvetic, March 1950, p. 2370; *Pittsburgh Press,* March 1, 31, 1950; *Pittsburgh Sun-Telegraph,* March 20, 1950; *The New York Times,* March 26, 1950. The following exchange took place between Cvetic and an IWO attorney at the decertification trial: "Q: Didn't you testify at the Un-American Activities Committee that it was 80 lbs.? A: [HUAC's] . . . agents . . . had to weigh them at the airport and they told me they were about 80 lbs . . . I think the total weight . . . was 93 lbs., but the documents themselves weighed about 80 lbs. . . . Q: You didn't see any contradiction between it saying 93 lbs. in one place and 80 lbs. in another? A: No" (IWO Trial Record, p. 2648). Notwithstanding all the hoopla about the either eighty or ninety-three pounds of material, a little over a year later HUAC returned it to Cvetic. He, in an attempt to reingratiate himself with a Pittsburgh Bureau that had kept him at arm's length, offered the material to the FBI. The cautious Pittsburgh Bureau agents wired Hoover's office for instructions on "whether the records should be accepted from Cvetic." The Pittsburgh FBI said, "This office is of the opinion that the material in Cvetic's possession probably is of little value." But the Pittsburgh FBI people also concluded that the mass of miscellaneous "leaflets, pamphlets, and several unidentified lists of names, etc." should be accepted, although "nothing of pertinent value" should be retained, in order "to eliminate any further use or dissemination of material by Cvetic." Hoover agreed and the Pittsburgh Bureau accepted the gift of the material and filed it away (FBI Pittsburgh to Director, FBI, May 25, 1951, pp. 2, 3; F. J. Baumgardner to A. H. Belmont, May 22, 1951; and FBI Pittsburgh to Director FBI, May 26, 1951–all in FBI Cvetic). A March 15, 1950 *Pittsburgh Press* headline read "Congressman Admits Giving Commie Group Free Ride on U.S." The newspaper's Washington Bureau ran down Congressman Sadowski, who "spoke out" through his office and admitted sending out a letter for the head of the American Slav Congress urging "free trade" between the United States and Communist China. The newspaper went on to point up the American Slav Congress's "pro-Communist stand," Sadowski's close relationship to the organization, and his frequent contributions to its journal.

18. Nelson, Barrett, and Ruck, *Steve Nelson,* p. 312; Nelson to Leab, September 20, 1990, p. 1.

19. Walter Goodman, *The Committee: The Extraordinary Career of the House Committee on Un-American Activities* (New York: Farrar, Straus & Giroux, 1968), p. 282; *Pittsburgh Press,* February 20, 1950; U.S. House of Representatives, Committee on Un-American Activities, *Annual Report . . . for 1950* (hereafter cited as "HUAC *Report* 1950"), p. 13. Six months before Cvetic approached HUAC, it had been holding hearings on the UE, and specifically Local 601. U.S. House of Representatives, Committee

on Un-American Activities, *Hearings Regarding Communist Infiltration of Labor Unions–Part I: Local 601, United Electrical, Radio, and Machine Workers of America, CIO, Pittsburgh, PA,* August 9–11, 1949. The "purpose of this hearing is to inquire into the questions of Communist affiliation or association of certain members of Local 601" (p. 541).

20. HUAC *Report* 1950, p. 13; Congressman Burr P. Harrison (D-Va.), HUAC Cvetic, March 1950, p. 1343; Nelson, *The 13th Juror,* p. 180; *Daily People's World,* April 30, 1951, p. 9; *Pittsburgh Press,* February 22, 1950; *Pittsburgh Post-Gazette,* February 22, 1950; Donner, *The Un-Americans,* p. 142. Vogeler served seventeen months of a fifteen-year sentence before the U.S. government could negotiate his release. Vogeler details how over seventy days "they broke me down," how in the "absence of any outside aid . . . my will to resist . . . was gradually . . . sapped" (Robert A. Vogeler, with Leigh White, *I Was Stalin's Prisoner* [New York: Harcourt, Brace, 1952], p. 182).

21. Joseph R. Starobin, *American Communism in Crisis, 1943–1951* (Cambridge: Harvard University Press, 1972), pp. 208–9.

22. *Pittsburgh Sun-Telegraph,* September 20, 1953. See Nelson, Barrett, and Ruck, *Steve Nelson,* p. 314.

23. *Pittsburgh Press,* February 28 and March 19, 1950.

24. *Pittsburgh Sun-Telegraph,* March ?, 1950*; Music News,* May 1950, quoted in Sarah B. McCall, "The Musical Fallout of Political Activism: Government Investigations of Musicians in the United States, 1930–1960" (Ph.D. diss., University of North Texas, 1993), p. 86; *Pittsburgh Post-Gazette,* May 18, 1950; *Pittsburgh Press,* June 27, 1950; Phillip Bonsky to Dan Leab, June 1, 1995; *Pittsburgh Post-Gazette,* March ?, 1950.

25. SAC Pittsburgh to Director FBI, March 2, 1950, FBI Cvetic; *Pittsburgh Post-Gazette,* March 6, 1950, and December 9, 1954; *Pittsburgh Press,* March 11, 1950. Cvetic named a married couple, who it turns out like Cvetic worked for the FBI. They did not surface until 1959. The wife recalls "when he named us it was the worst time in our lives. We thought about getting out, but the FBI asked us to stay and weather out the harassment." They did and on surfacing got a letter from Cvetic "congratulating us for our efforts" (Zaslow, "Red Scare," p. 82).

26. *Pittsburgh Press,* March 6, 1950; *Pittsburgh Sun-Telegraph,* March 6 and April 11, 1950.

27. Ronald Fillippelli and Mark D. McCulloch, *Cold War in the Working Class: The Rise and Decline of the United Electrical Workers* (Albany: SUNY Press, 1995), p. 143; "The Tragic Purge of 1948," *Bulletin for the Christian Remaking of Society,* February 1977, in Charles J. McCollester, ed., *Fighter with a Heart: Writings of Charles Owen Rice, Pittsburgh Labor Priest* (Pittsburgh: University of Pittsburgh Press, 1996), p. 97; Charles Owen Rice, "You Can Help Stop Reds in Labor Unions," *Our Sunday Visitor,* March 23, 1947, p. 1.

28. McCollester, *Fighter with a Heart,* p. 90; *Pittsburgh Sun-Telegraph,* March 20, 1950, clipping attached to SAC Pittsburgh to Director FBI, April 20, 1950, FBI Cvetic; interview with Monsignor Rice, August 16, 1988.

29. Interview with Sherman by [name deleted], report to Hyman Schlesinger, p. 1, *In the Case of Hyman Schlesinger,* UE Archives; Cvetic to Richard Arens, Senate Internal Security Subcommittee, November 14, 1953, quoted in Christopher John Gerard, " 'A Program of Cooperation': The FBI, the Senate Internal Security Subcommittee, and the Communist Issue, 1950–56" (Ph.D. diss., Marquette University, 1993), p. 229.

30. "Memorandum for the Director: Michael Angelo Musmanno," Febru-

ary 2, 1939, p. 2, FBI File no. 77–9685 (hereafter cited as "FBI Musmanno"); Michael A. Musmanno, *Verdict* (Garden City, N.Y.: Doubleday, 1958), p. 24.

31. Musmanno, *Verdict,* p. 31.

32. There is a carefully edited version of the letter in Nelson, *The 13th Juror,* p. 160; *Pittsburgh Post-Gazette,* March 20, 1951; Justin Kaplan, *Lincoln Steffens: A Biography* (New York: Simon & Schuster, 1974), p. 285; FBI Musmanno, p. 2. John Gunther, in an attempt to excuse the view of Mussolini he expressed in his various 1930s editions of *Inside Europe,* wrote in 1965 that "clearly I was taken in. . . . Well, so were a great many other people, including practically the entire British and American establishments of the period. . . . Even . . . Churchill admired the Duce. . . . So did Bernard Shaw [the playwright philosopher]. Those who saw through him . . . were dismissed as radical, eccentrics, or 'intellectuals.'. . . Mussolini began to slip in general esteem when he began to make an international nuisance of himself. . . . The invasion of Ethiopia in 1935 . . . the Fascist intervention in Spain and the formation of the Rome-Berlin Axis" (*Processions* [New York: Harper & Row, 1965], pp. 35–36).

33. Obituary, *Pittsburgh Post-Gazette,* October 13, 1968; Musmanno, *Verdict,* p. 356.

34. Musmanno, *Verdict,* pp. 329, 330; Melvin I. Urofsky, "Musmanno, Michael Angelo," *Dictionary of American Biography,* Supplement 8, "1966–1970," p. 456.

35. Musmanno, *Verdict,* p. 370; memorandum for the Assistant to the Attorney General Mr. Joseph B. Keenan, Re: Michael Angelo Musmanno, January 12, 1939, pp. 14, 15, 16, FBI Musmanno; Obituary, *Pittsburgh Post-Gazette,* October 13, 1968.

36. Memorandum for . . . Keenan [cited in full in previous note], January 12, 1939, pp. 15, 16, 17, FBI Musmanno.

37. "Bulletin Index, Pittsburgh PA," quoted in ibid., pp. 4–5.

38. *Current Biography,* p. 311.

39. The Associated Press dispatch quoted in ibid.; Henry Lea, "Nuremberg Trials: An Eyewitness Report," *Society for Exile Studies Infoblatt,* August 1998, p. 4. The "Einsatzgruppen" rampaged, terrorizing and killing, sometimes murdering "ethnic Germans whom they mistook for Jews" (Robert E. Condot, *Justice at Nuremberg* [New York: Harper & Row, 1983], pp. 211, 226–38).

40. Obituary, *Pittsburgh Post-Gazette,* October 13, 1968; R. A. Skelton et al., *The Vinland Map and the Tarter Relation* (New Haven: Yale University Press, 1965); Wilcomb Washburn, in "The World Before Columbus," February 13, 1996, transcript of an interview with Charlayne Hunter-Gault, *The MacNeill Lehrer Newshour* http://www.pbs.org/newshour/66/science/map_2-13.html; William Cullen Bryant and Sydney Howard Gay, *A Popular History of the United States from the First Discovery of the Western Hemisphere by the Northerners . . .* (New York: Charles Scribner's Sons, 1878), vol. 1, p. 41; *Pittsburgh Post-Gazette,* October 12, 1985; Michael A. Musmanno, *Columbus WAS First* (New York: Fountainhead Publishers, 1966); the *Yale Daily News,* with its customary arrogance, headlined its story on the publication of a second edition of The Vinland Map in 1996 "Yale Researchers Prove Vikings Were the First," notwithstanding the ongoing controversy (http://svensworld.com/vikings/ep61im/ vinland.html).

41. *Pittsburgh Press,* November 14, 1968; editorial, *Pittsburgh Press,* October 15, 1968; editorial, *Pittsburgh Post-Gazette,* October 18, 1968; Report, Pittsburgh, September 13, 1948, FBI Musmanno.

42. *The Daily Worker,* March 30, 1953; Michael A. Musmanno, *Across the Street from the Courthouse* (Philadelphia: Dorrance, 1954), p. 41; *Pittsburgh Post-Gazette,* March 30, 1953.

43. Typical are stories about Musmanno urging "Reds' internment," in *Pittsburgh Press,* July 22, 1950, and *Pittsburgh Post-Gazette,* July 24 and September 1, 1950.

44. Musmanno, *Across the Street,* p. 187; Nelson, *The 13th Juror,* pp. 181, 183.

45. Obituary, *Pittsburgh Press,* February 9, 1978; *Pittsburgh Post-Gazette,* May 24, 1961, and June 13 and December 12, 1951; *Pittsburgh Sun-Telegraph,* June 13, 1951.

46. *Pittsburgh Post-Gazette,* May 24, 1961. Schlesinger in a sense had the last laugh. As the *Pittsburgh Press* (March 17, 1978) reported, during the years of his travail he carefully invested in "corporate stocks" and "tax-free municipal and school bonds." At his death his estate totaled over $1,000,000.

47. IWO Trial Record, p. 2406; *Pittsburgh Post-Gazette,* April 7, 1951; IWO Trial Record, p. 2555.

48. V. P. Keay to H. B. Fletcher, February 27, 1950, FBI Cvetic; *Pittsburgh Press,* March 1, 1950.

49. I. F. Stone, "Story of a Victim of 2 Red-Scare Circus Stunts," *Daily Compass* (New York City), July 16, 1952.

Chapter 4

1. "Authority and Power of Attorney" (copy of the agreement between Cvetic, Moore, and Sherman), March 4, 1950, Frederic W. Ziv Papers, Department of Broadcasting, University of Cincinnati (hereafter cited as "Ziv Papers").

2. "Commonwealth of Pennsylvania vs. Steve Nelson," U.S. Supreme Court, *Records and Briefs,* vol. 62 (October term, 1955), pp. 769, 785; telephone interviews with James Moore, August 12 and September 26, 1988.

3. Tim Brooks and Earle Marsh, *The Complete Directory to PrimeTime Network and Cable TV Shows: 1946–Present* (New York: Ballantine Books, 1995), p. 1113; *We, the People* script, pp. 22, 23, *In the Case of Hyman Schlesinger,* UE Archives.

4. *We, the People* script, pp. 24, 26, 29, 28, *In the Case of Hyman Schlesinger,* UE Archives.

5. H. L. Edwards to W. R. Glavin, July 13, 1950, and Director FBI to FBI Pittsburgh, July 11, 1950, both in FBI Cvetic; IWO Trial Record, pp. 2664, 2665.

6. Mr. Jones to Mr. Nichols, July 17, 1950, p. 2, and L. B. Nichols to Mr. Tolson, July 17, 1950, both in FBI Cvetic. It is interesting to note that except for the pages concerning the immediate act of Cvetic's surfacing, the FBI seems to have released under FOIA almost all of the Bureau material on Cvetic to this point. But numerous pages were deleted from the material covering the next few years, during which the FBI tried to deal with the Cvetic "phenomenon."

7. John Tebbel and Mary Ellen Zuckerman, *The Magazine in America: 1741–1990* (New York: Oxford University Press, 1991), p. 145; Theodore H. White, *In Search of History: A Personal Adventure* (New York: Harper & Row, 1978), p. 399; telephone interviews with James Moore, August 12 and September 26, 1988; contract between Curtis Publishing Company and Cvetic, Sherman, and Moore, March 20, 1950 (copy), Ziv Papers.

8. Mr. A. H. Belmont to Mr. D. M. Ladd, July 20, 1950, pp. 1, 4, and August 2, 1980, p. 3, FBI Cvetic.

9. "Commonwealth of Pennsylvania vs. Steve Nelson," p. 755; IWO Trial Record, pp. 2610, 2616; Nelson, *The 13th Juror,* p. 185; Nelson to Leab, September 2, 1990, p. 2.

10. George Hickenlooper, *Reel Conversations: Candid Interviews with Film's Foremost Directors and Critics* (Secaucus, N.J.: Carol Publishing Group, 1991), p. 210; Robert Conquest, "In Celia's Office: Orwell and the Cold War," *Times Literary Supplement,* August 21, 1997, p. 5.

11. IWO Trial Record, p. 2573.

12. U.S. Chamber of Commerce, "Communism Within the Labor Movement," excerpt from a 1947 pamphlet quoted in L. K. Adler, "The Red Image: American Attitudes Toward Communism in the Cold War Era" (Ph.D. diss., University of California, Berkeley, 1971), p. 109.

13. "Agreement, August 9, 1950," *I Was a Communist for the FBI,* Ziv Papers; "Agreement Between Warner Brothers and the Frederic W. Ziv Company, December 3, 1951" (when I began researching the Cvetic story this agreement was in the Warner Brothers Archive, William Seymour Theatre Collection, Princeton University; since then that material has been transferred to WB USC); Daniel J. Leab, " 'The Iron Curtain': Hollywood's First Cold War Movie," *Historical Journal of Film, Radio, and Television,* no. 2 (1988): 187.

14. "Agreement, August 9, 1950," Ziv Papers; "Commonwealth of Pennsylvania vs. Steve Nelson," pp. 726, 864; Warner Brothers to Martin, August 9, 1950, WB USC.

15. *Variety,* August 8, 1950; *New York Times,* August 8, 1950; *Hollywood Reporter,* August 8, 1950; *Los Angeles Times,* August 8, 1950; and Lowell E. Redelings, "The Hollywood Scene," *Hollywood Citizen-News,* August 9, 1950, all from *I Was a Communist for the FBI,* clipping files, Academy of Motion Picture Arts and Sciences, Margaret Herrick Library (hereafter cited as "Clipping Files Herrick Library").

16. John Izod, *Hollywood and the Box Office, 1895-1986* (New York: Columbia University Press, 1988), p. 113; Ernest Borneman, "United States versus Hollywood," in Tino Balio, ed., *The American Film Industry,* rev. ed. (Madison: University of Wisconsin Press, 1985), p. 460.

17. Sklar, *Movie-Made America,* revised and updated (New York: Vintage Books, 1994), p. 274; Joel Finler, "New Channels for Movies," in Ann Lloyd et al., eds., *The Movies* (London: British Film Institute, 1980), p. 721; Truffaut quoted in J. Hoberman, *Vulgar Modernism: Writing on Movies and Other Media* (Philadelphia: Temple University Press, 1991), p. 7.

18. Kyle Crichton, "King of the B's," *Collier's,* January 7, 1939, pp. 23, 40; Joseph McBride, "Pioneer Film-Maker Bryan Foy Dies," *Daily Variety,* April 22, 1977, pp. 1, 16; *Paterson* [N.J.] *News,* January 13, 1961; "Bryan Foy: Putting the Picture on Film" (Warner Brothers press release, ca. 1951), pp. 2, 5, 6; "Biography–Bryan Foy" (Warner Brothers press release, March 1, 1957); Philip K. Scheuer, "Crane Wilbur, Star of Silent Film Carves Out New Career," *Los Angeles Times,* November 14, 1949, pp. 1, 3; "Screen Actor Wilbur Dies," *Los Angeles Times,* October 21, 1973, pt. 2, p. 8; and Ezra Goodman, "Crane Wilbur," *Los Angeles Daily News,* March 30, 1950, p. 20–all in Clipping Files Herrick Library.

19. Blake Lucas, "Bordon Chase," in Robert Morseberger et al., eds., *American Screenwriters* (Detroit: Gale Research, 1984), pp. 71–72; Leonard Maltin, "Gordon Douglas," *Action,* November–December 1970, p. 19; "Gordon Douglas–A Biography"

(Warner Brothers press release, no date), Clipping Files Herrick Library; Andrew Sarris, *The American Cinema* (New York: E. P. Dutton, 1969), p. 257.

20. Warner Brothers to Pete Martin, December 4, 1950; *Variety,* August 30, 1950, clipping, WB USC; "Frank Lovejoy—credits," compiled October 4, 1957, Clipping Files Herrick Library; Ephraim Katz, *The Film Encyclopedia* (New York: Perigee Books, 1982), pp. 810, 207; *New York Times Film Reviews: 1913–1968* (New York: Arno Press, 1970), appendix/index, p. 4348. Ever anxious to promote himself, Cvetic informed Pittsburgh newspapermen that James Cagney was "interested in playing . . . the screen Cvetic" (*Pittsburgh Sun-Telegraph,* August 22, 1950, clipping, WB USC).

21. Crane Wilbur, "Outline for *I Posed as a Communist for the FBI,*" WB USC.

22. Bordon Chase, "Treatment for *I Posed as a Communist for the FBI,*" October 21, 1950, cover; "I Posed as a Communist for the FBI," November 25, 1950, August 9, 1950, WB USC.

23. Chase, "Treatment for *I Posed as a Communist for the FBI,*" November 25, 1950, pp. 12, 24, 112, and December 9, 1950, p. 108, WB USC.

24. J. L. Warner to All Department Heads, November 11, 1950, WB USC. Jack Warner reported on the change to Martin and expressed certainty that it "will help in selling the picture." Warner to Martin, December 11, 1950, WB USC.

25. Wilbur, *I Was a Communist for the FBI,* script, December 22, 1950, WB USC.

26. Ibid., January 13, 1951, pp. 53–74; January 20, 1951, pp. 75–85 (revised); January 27, 1951, pp. 86–108; and February 5, 1941, pp. 108A–121 (revised); twenty revised pages, "Daily Production and Progress Sheets," *I Was a Communist for the FBI,* WB USC.

27. SAC Pittsburgh to Hoover, July 5, 1950; L. B. Nichols to Clyde Tolson, July 19 and September 6, 1950, and March 13, 1951; and SAC Letter No. 32, April 7, 1951, p. 10–all in FBI Cvetic. Interview with Jacques Kahn, Pittsburgh, August 16, 1988.

28. "Daily Production and Progress Sheets," H. J. McCord to J. H. Sporay (Ace Film Labs, Brooklyn, N.Y.), April 14, 1951, WB USC.

29. Wilbur, *I Was a Communist for the FBI,* January 27, 1951, p. 100; February 7, 1951, p. 119; and December 30, 1951, p. 16–all at WB USC. The script is cited here, but I also have drawn here and in following statements from a videotape of the film as broadcast on television (hereafter cited as " 'Communist' video").

30. Nelson to Leab, September 2, 1990.

31. Nelson, Barrett, and Ruck, *Steve Nelson,* pp. 3, 7, 20; obituary, *The New York Times,* December 14, 1993; Senate Judiciary Committee, "Steve Nelson," pp. 631, 632.

32. Theodore Draper, *American Communism and Soviet Russia,* with a new introduction and afterword (New York: Vintage Books, 1986), p. 455; Senate Judiciary Committee, "Steve Nelson," pp. 638, 641, 642. Among the books dealing with the Spanish Civil War or the battalion I looked at (and not all were favorable to the battalion) which mention Nelson are Vincent Brome, *The International Brigades: Spain–1936–1939* (London: Heineman, 1965); Peter N. Carroll, *The Odyssey of the Abraham Lincoln Brigade: Americans in the Spanish Civil War* (Stanford: Stanford University Press, 1994); Verle B. Johnson, *Legions of Babel: The International Brigades in the Spanish Civil War* (University Park: Pennsylvania State University Press, 1967); R. Dan Richardson, *The International Brigades and the Spanish Civil War* (Lexington: University Press of

Kentucky, 1982); Robert A. Rosenstone, *Crusade of the Left: The Lincoln Battalion in the Spanish Civil War* (New York: Pegasus, 1969); and Hugh Thomas, *The Spanish Civil War,* 2d ed. (London: Hanish Hamilton, 1977). Jason Gurney, *Crusade in Spain* (London: Faber & Faber, 1974), p. 137, makes some comments about Nelson and "secret trials," etc., which Nelson, Barrett, and Ruck dismiss because "Gurney had left Spain before Nelson ever arrived"; however, this is not the case. Gurney left Spain in August 1937 and Nelson took up his post just before May Day that year (pp. 204, 438nn.).

33. Nelson, Barrett, and Ruck, *Steve Nelson,* pp. 241, 251; Senate Judiciary Committee, "Steve Nelson," p. 666; Robert J. Lamphere and Tom Shachtman, *The FBI-KBG War: A Special Agent's Story* (1986; Macon, Ga.: Mercer University Press, 1995), p. 43: Hoover wrote FDR confidante and close aide Harry Hopkins in May 1943 that "a Russian . . . paid a sum of money to Steve Nelson . . . for the purpose of placing" CP members in industries "so that information would be obtained for transmittal to the Soviet Union" (Hoover to Hopkins, May 7, 1943, in Robert Louis Benson and Michael Warner, eds., *Soviet Espionage and the American Response 1939–1957* [Washington, D.C.: National Security Agency / Central Intelligence Agency, 1996], pp. 49–50). A former FBI agent testified along similar lines to a Senate committee in 1949. That testimony was reprinted in part in Senate Judiciary Committee, "Steve Nelson," which recorded Nelson's answer in 1948 at a hearing before a different congressional committee that "it might incriminate him if he answered questions as to whether he had ever been in the Soviet consulate, whether he had ridden in the automobile of the Soviet consulate in the period from 1938 to 1948" (p. 667). Years later Warren Olney III, the former assistant attorney general in charge of the Criminal Division of the Justice Department, recalled a conversation with Hoover over lunch. Hoover had spoken of how the tap on Nelson picked up not only what was said over the phone but also what was said in the room. According to Hoover, the bug had been planted not by the FBI but by Naval Intelligence, which worked with the Bureau from time to time. Agents did "tail" Nelson, recalled Olney, and saw him meet someone in the park across the street from the Soviet consulate to whom he handed something over (Warren Olney III, "Law Enforcement and Judicial Administration in the Early Warren Era," an oral history compiled from 1970 through 1977 by Marion F. Stern and Amelia R. Fry, Regional Oral History Office, The Bancroft Library, University of California, Berkeley, 1981, pp. 350–57).

34. Quoted in Senate Judiciary Committee, "Steve Nelson," p. 687.

35. Hosoon Chang, "National Security vs. First Amendment: U.S. Supreme Court Decisions on Anti-Communist Regulations, 1919–1974" (Ph.D. diss., University of North Carolina, Chapel Hill, 1993), p. 377; Sabin, *In Calmer Times,* p. 128; Milton R. Konvitz, *Expanding Liberties: The Emergence of New Civil Liberties and Civil Rights in Postwar America* (New York: Viking, 1967), p. 77; Melvin I. Urofsky, *The Continuity of Change: The Supreme Court and Individual Liberties, 1953–1986* (Belmont, Conn.: Wadsworth, 1991), p. 74; Alfred H. Kelly, Winifred A. Harbison, and Herman Belz, *The American Constitution: Its Origins and Development,* 6th ed. (New York: W. W. Norton, 1983), pp. 596–97; *Pittsburgh Press,* May 17, 1959.

36. *Pittsburgh Press,* March 16, 1953.

37. "The Incredible Informer and the Court," *Lawyers Guild Review,* Fall 1957, p. 89; quotation from Justice Warren decision in Mesarosh vs. U.S. (352 U.S. 156), in Chang, "National Security vs. First Amendment," pp. 387–88; U.S. Attorney

Malcolm Anderson, *Pittsburgh Post-Gazette,* September 14, 1957. Sherman defended Mazzei in a paternity suit in the fall of 1953. The Pittsburgh FBI SAC reported that the lawyer stated he was handling Mazzei as "a Commercial Attraction" and that he wanted him "to make some money as well as make money himself." Some months later interoffice correspondence in FBI headquarters in Washington, D.C., refers to Sherman's "exploiting" Cvetic, attempts to "muscle in" on Mazzei, and "to exploit him in the same manner as . . . Cvetic." Sherman would not work the same wonder twice (Fred Halford, SAC Pittsburgh, "Memorandum for the File," p. 2, October 14, 1953, and L. B. Nichols to Mr. Tolson, April 28, 1955, both in FBI Sherman).

38. William O. Douglas, *The Court Years 1939–1975* (New York: Random House, 1980), p. 92; Nelson, *The 13th Juror,* p. 18.

39. Nelson to Leab, September 2, 1990, p. 5; Nelson, Barrett, and Ruck, *Steve Nelson,* p. xii; Draper, *American Communism and Soviet Russia,* p. 456.

40. Quoted in obituary, *New York Times,* December 14, 1993; John Haynes and Harvey Klehn, *The American Communist Movement: Storming Heaven Itself* (New York: Twayne, 1992), p. 143; Nelson quoted in Maurice Isserman, *If I Had a Hammer . . . : The Death of the Old Left and the Birth of the New Left* (New York: Basic Books, 1987), p. 23.

41. Irving Howe, "The Great Seduction," *New Republic,* October 15, 1990, p. 47; Nelson, Barrett, and Ruck, *Steve Nelson,* p. 380; Nelson to Leab, September 2, 1990, p. 5; and Rice to Leab, February 25, 1995.

42. Quotations taken from the "dialogue transcript" for the trailer, WB USC.

43. "Communist" video. See also Wilbur, *I Was a Communist for the FBI,* December 30, 1950, pp. 33–34, 11–12, 20, 40, and January 17, 1951, p. 108, WB USC.

44. "Communist" video. See also Wilbur, *I Was a Communist for the FBI,* December 20, 1950, p. 78, and December 30, 1950, p. 24, WB USC. Scenes from the movie turn up in Cvetic, *The Big Decision,* p. 111 (murder of a defecting writer), p. 124 (leadership), and p. 156 ("third degree grillings by Party goons"). The scene about the CP fomenting racial discord particularly irritated Nelson, who wrote me, "What ever one thinks of the Communists, they were the first to fight to change the black situation in USA, i.e., of white org. . . . in USA" (Nelson to Leab, September 2, 1990, p. 3).

45. Nora Sayre, *Running Time: Films of the Cold War* (New York: Dial Press, 1982), p. 91; Michael Rogin, *Ronald Reagan, The Movie and Other Episodes in Political Demonology* (Berkeley and Los Angeles: University of California Press, 1987), p. 247. *Motion Picture Herald,* April 21, 1951; *Los Angeles Examiner,* April 28, 1951; *Time,* May 7, 1951; *Pittsburgh Post-Gazette,* April 20, 1951; Richard Griffith, " 'Communist for FBI' Called Formula Film," *Los Angeles Times,* May 15, 1951; T. Woodruff Smith to J. L. Warner, May 25, 1951; and *New Yorker,* May 12, 1951–all at WB USC.

46. J. L. Warner to Mort Blumenstock, April 7, 1951 (according to this telegram the "big quartet" are *Strangers on a Train, A Streetcar Named Desire, Captain Horatio Hornblower,* and *Jim Thorpe, All-American),* and *Motion Picture Herald,* July 7, 1951, both at WB USC.

47. *Newsweek,* May 14, 1951, clipping, WB USC. Pamphlet attached to Mort Blumenstock to J. L. Warner, May 3, 1951, WB USC.

48. Blumenstock to Bryan Foy, September 28, 1959; Blumenstock to Cvetic, March 22, 1951; and *Johnstown Democrat,* April 2, 3, 1951–all at WB USC. Interview with Jacques Kahn, August 16, 1988; Charles H. McCormack, *This Nest of*

Vipers: McCarthyism and Higher Education in the Mundel Affair, 1951–52 (Urbana: University of Illinois Press, 1989), p. 57.

49. Interview with Jacques Kahn, August 16, 1988, and L. B. Nichols to Clyde Tolson, April 16, May 1, 1951, both in FBI Cvetic.

50. Morleen Getz Rouse, "A History of the F. W. Ziv Radio and Television Syndication Companies, 1930–1960" (Ph.D. diss., University of Michigan, 1976), p. 151 (hereafter cited as "Ziv"); SAC Pittsburgh to Hoover, October 30, 1957, FBI Cvetic; "I Was a Communist for the FBI–Radio" (folder), WB USC; Maurice F. Koodish to Cvetic, October 22, 1951; complaint in the U.S. District Court for the Western Division, no. 4198, April 7, 1958; Koodish to Frederic W. Ziv, April 20, 1960, Ziv Papers.

51. Koodish to Ziv, December 8, 1951, Ziv Papers; "Commonwealth of Pennsylvania vs. Steve Nelson," pp. 762, 763, 785; *Pittsburgh Sun-Telegraph,* January 8, 1952, and *Pittsburgh Press,* May 26, 1957, FBI Cvetic; telephone interviews with James Moore, August 12 and September 16, 1988.

52. The television share of broadcast advertising dollars in "major markets" went from 32.7 percent in 1950 to 54.2 percent in 1952; the top radio program had a 26.3 rating in 1949 and only 8.5 in 1952. See J. Fred MacDonald, *One Nation Under Television: The Rise and Decline of Network TV* (New York: Pantheon, 1990), pp. 52–53. Isabel Selden, "The Ziv Reunion," *Emmy,* October 1986, pp. 70, 71; telephone interview with Frederic W. Ziv, August 3, 1990. *The* [Carter Oil Company] *Reporter,* vol. 1, no. 1, and Ziv sales plan used by Dayton, Ohio, American Legion, 1952, FBI Cvetic. Rouse, "Ziv," p. 152.

53. M. A. Jones to L. B. Nichols, April 15 and June 23, 1952, FBI Cvetic; Richard Gid Powers, *G-Man: Hoover's FBI in American Popular Culture* (Carbondale: Southern Illinois University Press, 1983), pp. 224–25; M. A. Jones to L. B. Nichols, April 1 and 8, June 23, and July 1, 1952, FBI Cvetic. Several of the shows are available on tape from Radio Spirits (Schiller Park, Ill.) but are misdated as being from the 1940s (e.g., "Jump to the Whip" and "Pennies from the Dead"). A lengthy excerpt from Script no. 76, "The Inhuman Element," is in Rouse, "Ziv," pp. 300–310.

54. Herbert Gordon, vice-president, Ziv Radio Productions, to Hoover, October 22, 1951; Hoover to Gordon, October 30, 1951; SAC Pittsburgh to L. B. Nichols, January 22, 1952; and Hoover to Gordon, January 25, 1952–all in FBI Cvetic. Ziv quoted in J. Fred MacDonald, *Television and the Red Menace: The Video Road to Vietnam* (New York: Praeger, 1985), p. 103. The company's statement is in L. B. Nichols to Clyde Tolson, January 30, 1952, SAC Letter no. 13, March 14, 1952, FBI Cvetic.

55. Trendle-Campbell Broadcasting Corp. to Hoover, March 13, 1952; SAC Houston to Hoover, March 15, 1952; L. B. Nichols to Clyde Tolson, March 18, 1952; [name deleted] to Hoover, April 20, 1952; Hoover to [name deleted], April 26, 1952; [name deleted] to Hoover, May 23, 1952; Hoover to [name deleted], June 2, 1952; SAC Dallas to Hoover, June 10, 1952; *Fort Worth Star-Telegram,* May 29, and June 4 and 5, 1952; L. L. Laughlin to A. H. Belmont, July 23, 1952 (on which there is a note from Hoover that "we want no part in Cvetic's promotion"); A. Mohr to Tolson, September 25, 1952; [name deleted] to Hoover, April 30, 1952; *Pittsburgh Press,* April 12, 1953; Hoover to [name deleted], May 8, 1953; [name deleted,] Rawlins, N.Y., to Nichols, July 22, 1953; and Nichols to [name deleted,] Rawlins, N.Y., July 27, 1953– all in FBI Cvetic. According to the rate schedules for *I Was a Communist for the FBI* (1952), Ziv Papers, the cost of the program to broadcasters for the series initially was:

Market Population		Cost
Under	10,000	$13.00 each
	15,000	15.50
	25,000	22.50
	35,000	28.50
	50,000	37.50
	75,000	53.50
	100,000	63.50
	150,000	73.50
	250,000	92.50
	375,000	110.00
	500,000	139.50
	750,000	157.50
	1,000,000	192.50
Philadelphia		250.00
Los Angeles		300.00
Chicago		350.00
New York City		500.00

Lawrence and Lee actually produced the series, with Ziv advancing production costs and retaining 90 percent of the gross until these had been recouped. Thereafter, an increased percentage of the gross went to Lawrence and Lee (see Rouse, "Ziv," p. 151).

56. Rouse, "Ziv," p. 171; Michael Kackman, "Citizen, Communist, Counterspy: *I Led Three Lives* and Television's Masculine Agent of History," *Cinema Journal* 38 (Fall 1998): 111–sadly though the author makes some very interesting points he misspells Cvetic's name as "Cvetik"; SAC Pittsburgh to Hoover, July 27, 1953, FBI Cvetic.

Chapter 5

1. Donner, *The Un-Americans,* p. 146; Caute, *The Great Fear,* p. 200; Nelson, *The 13th Juror,* p. 204.

2. Donner, *The Un-Americans,* p. 146; SAC Pittsburgh to the Director, June 1, 1950, p. 2, March 13, 1950, p. 28, FBI Cvetic.

3. *Washington News,* March 20, 1950, clipping attached to Director FBI to SAC Pittsburgh, April 7, 1950; SAC Pittsburgh to Director FBI, April 20, 1950; and advertisement for "Conspiracy," a pamphlet by Cvetic, c. 1960, *San Diego Union,* July 29, 1960–all in FBI Cvetic. Donner, "The Informer," p. 307; H. H. Clegg to Clyde Tolson, October 15, 1952, FBI Cvetic.

4. D. M. Ladd to the Director, February 3, 1953, p. 1; A. H. Belmont to Mr. Ladd, February 6, 1953; C. H. Hennrich to A. H. Belmont, February 9, 1953, p. 2–all in FBI Cvetic.

5. Note appended to Hoover to SAC Pittsburgh, September 4, 1952; Mr. A. H. Belmont to Mr. D. M. Ladd, March 7, 1953; A. H. Belmont to Mr. Ladd, February 6, 1953; handwritten comment on Mr. D. M. Ladd to the Director, February 3, 1953, p. 3 (obviously written a day or two later); and L. L. Laughlin to A. H. Belmont, July 23, 1952–all in FBI Cvetic. D. M. Ladd to Hoover, February 17, 1953, FBI Cvetic, is a multipage review of the Bureau's comments about Cvetic to government attorneys and others in the Department of Justice. On page 3 is what seems to be

Hoover's handwritten comment, "We certainly have done our duty in alerting Dep. J. as to Cvetic," which may be the reason for the review.

6. William F. Tompkins, Assistant Attorney General, Internal Security Division, to Director, Federal Bureau of Investigation, June 12, 1956, Departmental Committee on Security Witnesses, Minutes of Meeting of July 7, 1955, p. 2, U.S. Department of Justice, no. CRM-890912F (hereafter cited as "Justice Cvetic").

7. Robert Griffith, *The Politics of Fear: Joseph R. McCarthy and the Senate,* 2d ed. (Amherst: University of Massachusetts Press, 1987), p. 117; Sabin, *In Calmer Times,* p. 129; Alan D. Harper, *The Politics of Loyalty: The White House and the Communist Issue, 1946–1952* (Westport, Conn.: Greenwood Publishing Corporation, 1969), pp. 277, 278, 291.

8. Harper, *Politics of Loyalty,* pp. 284, 285; Fried, *Nightmare in Red,* p. 118;

9. Caute, *The Great Fear,* p. 178; Paul Buhle, "Young Communist League (and Successors)," in Buhle, Mary Jo Buhle, and Dan Georgakas, eds., *Encyclopedia of the American Left* (New York: Garland Publishing, 1990), pp. 872, 874; Departmental Committee on Security Witnesses, Minutes of Meeting of April 21, 1955, p. 2, Justice Cvetic.

10. Departmental Committee on Security Witnesses, Minutes of Meeting of April 21, 1955, Justice Cvetic; opinion quoted in Warren Olney III, Assistant Attorney General, Criminal Division, Department of Justice, to Director, Federal Bureau of Investigation, June 15, 1955, Justice Cvetic.

11. David L. Rosenberg, "The Red Scare and Pittsburgh Jewry," *Jewish Chronicle* (Pittsburgh), July 9, 1992; *Digest of the Public Record of Communism in the United States,* p. 169; Caute, *The Great Fear,* p. 229; Jenkins, *The Cold War at Home,* p. 205.

12. Hoover, memorandum for Mr. Tolson, Mr. Boardman, Mr. Belmont, and Mr. Nichols, April 5, 1955, p. 4, FBI Cvetic; IWO Trial Record, p. 2324. Thornton, SAC Pittsburgh, to Charles Garfinkel, March 2, 1950; SAC Pittsburgh to Director FBI, March 2, 15, 1950; Director FBI to the Commissioner, Immigration and Naturalization Service, March 15, 1950; and Director FBI to SAC Pittsburgh, March 16, 1950, p. 3–all in FBI Cvetic. *Pittsburgh Press,* March 1, 1950. Pirinsky, erstwhile executive secretary of the American Slav Congress, reported a subsequent official "left the United States in August of 1951 as a result of deportation proceedings brought against him. . . ." ("Attorney General v. American Slav Congress," Docket No. 112–53, *Reports of the Subversive Activities Board,* Vol. ii (Washington, D.C.: Government Printing Office, 1960), p. 571).

13. IWO Trial Record, p. 2386; "Immigration Service Re: Charles Soldo . . . 4/8/54 through 4/12/54–Excerpts from cross-examination in official Transcript and Testimony of Matt Cvetic," p. 87, *In the Case of Hyman Schlesinger,* UE Archives; Mr. D. M. Ladd to the Director, November 12, 1952, FBI Cvetic.

14. "Immigration Service Re: Charles Soldo," pp. 3, 2, 9.

15. Garfinkel to Mr. K. I. Zimmerman, District Director, Philadelphia, Pa., November 19, 1952, U.S. Department of Justice, Immigration and Naturalization Service no. C 2.12-C/CO893420 (hereafter cited as "INS Cvetic").

16. Commissioner of Immigration and Naturalization to the Attorney General, no date–c. February 1955, INS Cvetic.

17. "Immigration Service Re: Charles Soldo," pp. 16, 15.

18. John W. McIlvaine, U.S. Attorney, Pittsburgh, to William F. Tompkins, Assistant Attorney General, Internal Security Division, Department of Justice, April 4,

1955, pp. 1, 2, Executive Office for United States Attorneys no. 90–0810-R (hereafter cited as "EOUSA").

19. *Daily Worker,* March 31 and April 13, 1955; press release in Director FBI to the Attorney General, March 31, 1955, pp. 4–5; FBI Pittsburgh to the Attorney General, March 9, 1955, p. 2; Director FBI to the Attorney General, March 9, 1955; and A. H. Belmont to L. V. Boardman, March 8 (Hoover comment also asks "where have they been") and 11, 1955–all in FBI Cvetic.

20. Herbert Brownell, Jr., Attorney General, to Messers. Rogers, Hoover, Swino, Rankin, Tompkins, and Olney, March 21, 1955, p. 3, and SAC Pittsburgh to Director FBI, June 15, 1955, p. 11, both in FBI Cvetic. McIlvaine to Tompkins, April 4, 1955, p. 3, EOUSA; FBI Pittsburgh to Director FBI, April 6, 1955, FBI Cvetic.

21. SAC Pittsburgh to Director FBI, May 6, 1955, FBI Cvetic; Donner, *The Un-Americans,* p. 147; Mr. A. H. Belmont to Mr. L. V. Boardman, October 14, 1955, FBI Cvetic.

22. "Brief Statement on the John J. Mullen Attack on Justice Michael H. Musmanno" [probably by Matt Cvetic], c. April 1953, Musmanno Papers. Much is made in the release of former FBI plant Joseph Mazzei's affidavit concerning Mullen, but it is important to realize that Mazzei proved even less credible than Cvetic. A man of little repute, accused of being a pedophile, Mazzei had been caught lying from the moment he surfaced. In relying on his affidavit, those attacking Mullen were using a *very* weak reed. In March 1954 Cvetic also made out an affidavit in which he made various allegations about Mullen—none deal with any time after 1948; all are vague. The most damming thing Cvetic could say was that "the Communist Party could depend on him" to support certain issues, but it may well have been that those issues were ones onto which the CP latched. Cvetic's affidavit, like his testimony, is unclear. "Affidavit by Matthew Cvetic," March ?, 1954, p. 4, Musmanno Papers.

23. George P. Spine, Assistant, Officer in Charge, FBI Pittsburgh 19, Pennsylvania, to Garfinkel, June 13, 1955, INS Cvetic. How this came to me, I am not certain: the cover letter that went with the document quoted a reference that "asked that the information be denied" (Verna Tynes for M. S. Ortiz, Chief/PA Section, U.S. Department of Justice, Immigration and Naturalization Service, February 9, 1994, to Leab); on the Spine letter is the notation "HQINU recommends this page *not* be released . . . October 18, 1993."

24. *Pittsburgh Sun-Telegraph,* August 23, 1953, in SAC Pittsburgh to Director FBI, August 27, 1953, FBI Cvetic; Labor Research Association, *Labor Fact Book 12* (New York: International Publishers, 1955), p. 72.

25. Murray Kempton, *America Comes of Middle Age* (Boston: Little, Brown, 1963), p. 25; Senate Judiciary Committee, Subcommittee to Investigate the Administration of the Internal Security Act, *Hearings on Communist Underground Printing Facilities and Illegal Propaganda,* 83d Congress, 1st sess., July 10, 1953, p. 335 (in this hearing Cvetic did not prove as fast on the uptake as he should have been concerning Taylor, and the senator actually had to press him), and *Hearings* on *Communist Propaganda,* 83d Congress, 2d sess., October 7, 1954, p. 68. Cvetic had such an impact that in 1957 during the Democratic primary a special issue of *The Democrat,* Taylor's campaign sheet, devoted over a page to exposing Cvetic with materials supplied by Schlesinger (*The Democrat,* Taylor to Schlesinger, July 17, 1957, *In the Case of Hyman Schlesinger,* UE Archives).

26. L. B. Nichols to Mr. Tolson, July 19, 1950, FBI Cvetic; *Pittsburgh Sun-*

Telegraph, January 7, 1952; *Pittsburgh Press,* January 8, 1952; Donner, "The Informer," p. 307.

27. "Matthew Cvetic," November 22, 1954, p. 1, FBI Cvetic; *The Democrat,* p. 1; *Pittsburgh Press,* August 31, 1951.

28. *Pittsburgh Post-Gazette,* April 15, 1953, and January 18, 1954; *Pittsburgh Sun-Telegraph,* February 23, 1954; and Pittsburgh Press, April 11, 1954–all in FBI Cvetic. "Address by Matthew Cvetic, Republican Candidate for Congress, Twenty-Eighth Pennsylvania District," Radio Station WCAC, Saturday, April 10, 1954–6:05 p.m., inscribed to "To My Good Friend, the Judge" by Matt Cvetic, Musmanno Papers.

29. FBI Salt Lake City to Director FBI, July 22, 1955; to Communications Section, for SAC, Salt Lake City, July 20, 1955–both in FBI Cvetic.

30. Mr. A. Rosen to Mr. Michaels, October 3, 1955; Mr. A. H. Belmont to Mr. L. V. Boardman, July 5, 1955; Mr. F. J. Baumgardner to Mr. A. H. Belmont, July 25, 1955; and memorandum to Boardman from Belmont, re: Matthew Cvetic, July 5, 1955–all in FBI Cvetic. Albert E. Kahn, *The Matusow Affair: Memoir of a National Scandal,* introduction by Angus Cameron (Mt. Kisco, N.Y.: Moyer Bell, 1987), p. xix.

31. Senate Judiciary Committee, Subcommittee to Investigate the Administration of the Internal Security Act, *Hearings on Strategy and Tactics of World Communism (The Significance of the Matusow Case),* 84th Congress, 1st sess., pp. 2, 282, 284.

32. Mr. A. H. Belmont to Mr. L. V. Boardman, August 9, 1955, and SAC Salt Lake City to Director FBI, August 13, 1955, both in FBI Cvetic.

33. *Las Vegas Review-Journal,* July 17, 1955, clipping attached to SAC, Pittsburgh to Director FBI (ATTN: Mr. Belmont), July 19, 1955, and John Cahlan to Hoover, July 12, 1955, both in FBI Cvetic.

34. Cvetic to Musmanno, August 24, 1955 and Friday, [date deleted,] 1955, Musmanno Papers; *Las Vegas Independent,* December 1, 1955, clipping, Musmanno Papers; [name deleted], Beverly Hills, Calif., to [name deleted], in [place-name deleted], Administrative Assistant to Nichols, February 15, 1956, FBI Cvetic.

35. SAC Pittsburgh to Director FBI, May 28 and October 18, 1956, FBI Cvetic.

36. Cvetic quoted in SAC Pittsburgh to Director FBI, March 10, 1955, pp. 1, 2, and Director FBI to SAC Pittsburg [*sic*], April 5, 1955, both in FBI Cvetic.

37. John Tebbel, *A History of Book Publishing in the United States,* vol. 3, *The Golden Age Between Two Wars, 1920–1940* (New York: R. R. Bowker, 1978), p. 545; Edward S. Dangel to Musmanno, March 10, 1955, Musmanno Papers; L. C. Page and Co. to Justice Michael Musmanno, May 31, 1955, Musmanno Papers; Tebbel, p. 545.

38. Matt Cvetic, "They Call Me Comrade," manuscript, chap. 3: "I'm a Communist for the FBI," pp. 1, 7. There are also other chapters in the Musmanno Papers.

39. Cvetic, *The Big Decision,* pp. iii, 8, 12.

40. Ibid., pp. 28, 47, 91n.; Mr. Baumgardner to Mr. Belmont, August 31, 1960, FBI Cvetic.

41. FBI Pittsburgh to Director (Attention of Assistant Director A. H. Belmont), April 6, 1956, p. 1, and Mr. A. H. Belmont, April 5, 1956, both in FBI Cvetic.

42. J. A. Sizod to A. H. Belmont, April 5, 1956, and FBI Pittsburgh to Director (Attention of Assistant Director A. H. Belmont), April 6, 1956, pp. 2–4, both in FBI Cvetic; telephone interview with Ziv, August 5, 1990.

43. Powers, *Secrecy and Power,* p. 305. It was as Powers argues, a no-lose situ-

ation for Hoover. If the person "was subsequently unfriendly to the Bureau, that validated Hoover's judgement." If the person was friendly, "it proved his sincerity." A. H. Belmont to L. V. Boardman, October 10, 1957; SAC Pittsburgh to Director FBI, April 30, 1958; Director FBI to FBI Los Angeles, May 15, 1958; A. H. Belmont to L. V. Boardman, May 28, 1958; Cvetic to Hoover, February 24, March 19, and September 14, 1958; Francis Case (R-SD) to Hoover, March 4, 1959; and Hoover to Case, March 10, 1959–all in FBI Cvetic.

44. Cvetic to [name deleted], December 6, 1956; SAC New York to Director FBI, December 31, 1956; FBI Pittsburgh to Director FBI, January 14, 1957, p. 1; Hoover to SAC Pittsburgh, January 15, 1957; and SAC Pittsburgh to Director FBI, January 28, 1957, p. 1–all in FBI Cvetic.

45. SAC Pittsburgh to Director FBI, January 28, 1957, pp. 1, 2, 5, and SAC Pittsburgh to Director FBI, February 6, 1957, p. 3, both in FBI Cvetic.

46. L. B. Nichols to Mr. Tolson, February 14, 1957, FBI Cvetic.

47. L. B. Nichols to Mr. Tolson, February 18, 1957; Cvetic quoted in SAC Pittsburgh to Director FBI, April 11, 1957, pp. 1–2; and Mr. Nichols to Mr. Tolson and Director, February 1, 1957–all in FBI Cvetic.

48. Although the name is blacked out, it is clear that the exchange involved Govorchin. Govorchin to Federal Bureau of Investigation, August 10, 1959, and Hoover to Govorchin, August 18, 1959, both in FBI Cvetic; Govorchin, *Americans from Yugoslavia,* pp. 247–51.

49. SAC Pittsburgh to Director FBI, April 11, 1957, FBI Cvetic; *Pittsburgh Press,* May 26, 1957.

50. Mr. A. H. Belmont to Mr. L. V. Boardman, October 10, 1957, p. 1; note on Cvetic to Editor, *Pittsburgh Sun-Telegraph,* October 6, 1957; Cvetic to the American Legion Convention, September 17, 1957; copy, SAC Pittsburgh to Director FBI, January 15, 1958, p. 2–all in FBI Cvetic.

51. Cvetic to Musmanno, March 16, 1959, Musmanno Papers; SAC Pittsburgh to Director FBI, January 21, 1958, p. 1, FBI Cvetic.

52. SAC Pittsburgh to Director FBI, January 21, 1958, p. 2, and SAC Pittsburgh to Director FBI, February 24, 1958, both in FBI Cvetic.

53. Cvetic to Musmanno, May 1, February 28, and August 7, 1958, Musmanno Papers; Director FBI to SAC Los Angeles, February 11, 1959, attachment no. 2, FBI Cvetic.

54. Cvetic to Musmanno, February 28, 1958, Musmanno Papers. *Rapid City Daily Journal,* June 16, 1959, clipping attached to SAC Pittsburgh to Hoover, July 1, 1959, and Director FBI to SAC Los Angeles, February 11, 1959, attachment no. 2, both in FBI Cvetic. The rest of the fee schedule was:

50,000 to 100,000	$300
100,000 and over	$350
State conventions, conferences, and other events	$350
National conventions, conferences, and other events	Fees on request

Cvetic to Musmanno, November 14, 1958, Musmanno Papers; [name deleted], Department of Public Utilities, City of Saint Paul, St. Paul, Minn., to Hoover, April 21, 1959, FBI Cvetic.

55. Benjamin R. Epstein and Arnold Forster, *The Radical Right: Report on the John Birch Society and Its Allies* (New York: Random House, 1967), p. 3; Brooks R. Walker, *The Christian Fright Peddlers* (Garden City, N.Y.: Doubleday, 1964); Daniel

Bell, ed., *The Radical Right: The New American Right—Expanded and Updated* (Garden City, N.Y.: Anchor Books, 1964), p. 12n.; *Big Decision* brochure attached to SAC Pittsburgh to Director FBI, September 30, 1960, and calling card attached to SAC Pittsburgh to Director FBI, July 13, 1959, both in FBI Cvetic.

56. Epstein and Forster, *Radical Right,* p. 32; SAC Pittsburgh to Director FBI, April 13, 1961, FBI Cvetic; Cvetic to Musmanno, November 1, 1961, Musmanno Papers; Arnold Forster and Benjamin R. Epstein, *Danger on the Right* (New York: Random House, 1964), p. 9; N. P. Callahan to the Director, March 6, 1962, FBI Cvetic (Rousselot entered other Cvetic articles as well—e.g., N. P. Callahan to Hoover, June 25, 1962, FBI Cvetic, dealing with "Extremists"; N. P. Callahan to Hoover, July 25, 1962, FBI Cvetic, dealing with "Communism in Our Churches").

57. [Name deleted], Agra, Kansas, May 19, 1961; *San Diego Tribune,* July 28, 1960; SAC San Diego to Director FBI (Attention: Assistant Director Al Belmont), August 1, 1960—all in FBI Cvetic.

58. Forster and Epstein, *Danger on the Right,* p. 79; Matt Cvetic, "The Mental Health Goldbrick," *The American Mercury,* January 1960, pp. 223–26; interview, "Matt Cvetic Focuses Spotlight on Communist Activities Throughout the Country," *The Carpenteria Herald,* enclosure with SAC Los Angeles to Director FBI, March 28, 1961, FBI Cvetic; Hans Engh, "The John Birch Society," *The Nation,* March 11, 1961, p. 211.

59. Fred J. Cook, *The Nation,* June 30, 1962 (Special Issue), p. 571, and "Reds Swarming Here, Ex-FBI Agent Warns," *Los Angeles Times,* July 27, 1959, attachment to SAC Los Angeles to Director FBI, July 27, 1959; C. D. DeLoach to Mr. Tolson, July 27, 1959; and SAC Los Angeles to Director FBI, July 29, 1959—all in FBI Cvetic.

60. "George Todt's Opinion," *Los Angeles Herald-Express,* February 27, 1961, enclosure with Todt to Hoover, March 4, 1951 (although the name is blacked out, the sender seems to be Todt), FBI Cvetic; obituaries, *Los Angeles Herald-Examiner,* July 27, 1962, and the *New York Times,* July 27, 1962; Zaslow, "Red Scare," p. 67.

Epilogue: A Cautionary Tale

1. *Newsweek,* August 6, 1962, p. 57; Hoover to [name deleted], Amarillo, Tex., August 14, 1962; and Hoover to [name deleted], Granada Hills, Calif., October 11, 1962—all in FBI Cvetic.

2. Zaslow, "Red Scare," p. 67; brochure, "Matt Cvetic 100% American," enclosed with SAC Los Angeles to Director FBI, March 6, 1963, and SAC, Los Angeles to Director, FBI, August 3, 1962, both in FBI Cvetic.

3. Arthur M. Schlesinger, "Extremism in American Politics," *Saturday Review,* November 27, 1965, p. 24.

4. Senate Judiciary Committee, Subcommittee to Investigate the Administration of the Internal Security Act, *Hearings on Communist Propaganda,* pt. 2, 83d Congress, 2d sess., October 7, 1954, p. 77; Schrecker, *Many Are the Crimes,* p. 173.

5. Trumbo, quoted in Victor S. Navasky, *Naming Names* (New York: Viking Press, 1980), p. 387; Jenkins, *The Cold War at Home,* p. 18.

6. Rice to Leab, October 7, 1988, p. 2, and February 25, 1995; interview with Rice, August 16 1988.

7. John Lewis Gaddis, *We Now Know: Rethinking Cold War History* (Oxford: Clarendon Press, 1997, p. 27 (emphasis in original).

8. Peter H. Buckingham, *America Sees Red: Anticommunism in America:*

1870s to 1980s—A Review of Issues and References (Claremont, Calif.: Regina Books, 1988), p. xii.

9. Willie Morris, *New York Days* (Boston: Little, Brown, 1993), p. 50; John Earl Haynes, *Red Scare or Red Menace: American Communism and Anticommunism in the Cold War Era* (Chicago: Ivan R. Dee, 1996), p. 189. Haynes seems to me correct in his analysis, however, that even in the midst of this increasingly voluble anti-Communist hullabaloo that many Americans continued to regard Communism as they "regard all politics and politicians—just one of the many sideshows in life" (Haynes to Leab, November 18, 1990); Jenkins, *The Cold War at Home,* p. 7.

10. Guenter Lewy, *The Cause That Failed: Communism in American Life* (New York: Oxford University Press, 1990), p. 78; Stanley I. Kutler, foreword to Stephen J. Whitfield, *The Culture of the Cold War,* 2d ed. (Baltimore: Johns Hopkins University Press), pp. viii, 4; Caute, *The Great Fear,* pp. 17, 216–23; Fried, *Nightmare in Red,* p. 164; M. J. Heale, *American Anti-Communism: Combating the Enemy Within, 1930–1970* (Baltimore: Johns Hopkins University Press, 1990), p. 183.

11. Alsop quoted in Elizabeth Bentley, *Out of Bondage: KGB Target, Washington, DC* (1951; New York: Ivy Books, 1988), p. 218.

12. Lionel Trilling, "Whittaker Chambers and 'The Middle of the Journey,' " *New York Review,* April 17, 1975, p. 23; Sam Tanenhaus, *Whittaker Chambers* (New York: Random House, 1997), p. 504; Allen Weinstein, *Perjury: The Hiss-Chambers Case* (1978; New York: Random House, 1997), p. 513—the new edition "was reshaped with page-by-page revisions . . . and the addition of a substantially new final chapter that brings . . . the case up to the present" (p. xi).

13. Philbrick, *I Led Three Lives.*

14. Whitfield, *Culture of the Cold War,* p. 66; John Earl Haynes and Harvey Klehr, *Venona: Decoding Soviet Espionage in America* (New Haven: Yale University Press, 1999), p. 278.

15. Selma R. Williams, *Red Listed: Haunted by the Washington Witch Hunt* (Reading, Mass.: Addison-Wesley, 1994), p. xii. This book is very much of a type. Yet it is better than most, which is why I cite it, because of her interviews with some dozen people who were affected. Unfortunately, it seems to me she turns a blind eye to at least some of what they are saying, which in the context of their time and perhaps ours leaves them less innocent than Ms. Williams supposes and would have us believe.

16. Lamphere and Shachtman, *FBI-KGB War,* p. 19.

17. Schrecker, *Many Are the Crimes,* p. 140.

18. *Pittsburgh Post,* May 26, 1957.

19. David Rosenberg, "The Red Scare and Pittsburgh Jewry," pt. 2, *The Jewish Chronicle of Pittsburgh,* July 16, 1992, p. 9; Zaslow, "Red Scare," p. 69.

20. Oakes, quoted in Bayley, *Joe McCarthy and the Press,* p. 216; *Pittsburgh Post-Gazette,* October 22, 1954, December 8, 1956.

21. Zaslow, "Red Scare," pp. 67, 68.

22. Ibid., p. 72.

23. Telephone interview with Steve Nelson, September 8, 1988.

24. Goebbels, quoted in David Welch, "Powers of Persuasion," *History Today,* August 1999, p. 26.

25. Costa-Gavras, quoted in Hickenlooper, *Reel Conversations,* p. 108.

Index

Abraham Lincoln Battalion, 83–84, 88
Adamic, Louis, 5
Adler, Larry, 108
Adler, Lee, 75
Albert, Dorothy, 58
Alcoholics Anonymous, Cvetic's
    membership in, 104–5
Allen, Steve, 122
Allis Chalmers, 10
Alsop, Joseph, 130
American Civil Liberties Union, 29–30
American Legion, 119
American Mercury, The, 122
American Newspaper Guild, 35
Americans Battling Communism, Inc.,
    44–47, 51–52, 71, 147n.37
American Slav, The, 8
American Slav Congress, 21, 134,
    145nn.20–21, 148n.17
    formation of, 17–18
    investigation of, 37–39
    Nelson and, 80
    Sherman's campaign against, 55–56
Andrews, Dana, 93–94
anti-Communism in U.S.
    decline of, 119–20
    impact on Cvetic's career of, 128–29
    increased visibility of, 33–34, 129n.9
    movie industry exploitation of, 77–78
    "premature" phase of, 29
    witch hunts prompted by, 131–32
atomic espionage investigations, 32,
    84–85, 144n.8

Bagehot, Walter, 38
Barbers' License Bill, 63
Barcoski, John, 63
Barsh, Anna M., 8–9
Barsh, Barbara, 8
Barsh, Marie Dolores, 7–8
Bentley, Elizabeth, 111, 130
Berlin Blockade, 31, 132
Bianco, Anthony F., 41
Big Decision, The, 114–15, 117, 121, 125,
    137n.4
Black Fury, 63
Braden, Carl and Anne, 108
Bryant, William Cullen, 66
Buckingham, Peter, 128
Budenz, Louis, 50, 130

Cahlan, John, 112
Calomiris, Angela, 11, 35, 130
Carey, Philip, 79
Carlson, Richard, 131
Carter Oil Company, 93–94
Catholic Church, anti-Communism in,
    22
Caute, David, 19, 102, 129
Chambers, Whittaker, 32, 130–31
Chase, Bordon, 78–80
China, Communist takeover of, 31
Christian Crusade, 3, 121–22, 126
Christian Science Monitor, 90
Civil Rights Congress, 99–101
Clark, Mark (General), 65
Coal and Iron Police, 63–64